Reverse
Glass Painting

Reverse Glass Painting

Tips, Tools, and Techniques for Learning the Craft

ANNE DIMOCK

Photography by Kevin Brett

STACKPOLE
BOOKS

To Margaret "Peg" Emery

My teacher, mentor, and wonderful Christian friend,
who has shared her passion and knowledge
of reverse glass painting with me for more than
three decades. Thank you, my dear friend.

Published by
STACKPOLE BOOKS
5067 Ritter Road
Mechanicsburg, PA 17055
www.stackpolebooks.com

Printed in China

10 9 8 7 6 5 4 3 2 1

FIRST EDITION

Cover design by Tracy Patterson

Frontispiece: Empire looking glass by Anne Dimock showing
a festive scene surrounded by a stenciled and gold-leaf border.

Library of Congress Cataloging-in-Publication Data

Dimock, Anne, 1946–
     Reverse glass painting : tips, tools, and techniques for
  learning the craft / Anne Dimock ; photography by Kevin
  Brett. — 1st ed.
        p.   cm.
     Includes bibliographical references.
     ISBN-13: 978-0-8117-0522-6 (pbk.)
     ISBN-10: 0-8117-0522-6 (pbk.)
     1. Glass painting and staining.   2. Glass underpainting.
  I. Title.

TT298.D485   2010
748.5—dc22

2009028673

CONTENTS

ACKNOWLEDGMENTS

This book could not have become a reality without the help and encouragement of many people. Linda Brubaker began the process by telling me about the Stackpole Books crafts series and introducing me to Kyle Weaver, who agreed to make it happen.

I am deeply indebted to my mentor and teacher, Peg Emery, for being so willing to share her knowledge of reverse glass painting with me. Without her, there would be no book. My daughter Stephanie performed all the computer work for me, putting up with my endless need to change things around. My friend and student Linda Mason read and reread the manuscript, helping to make it all make sense. They both have my deep gratitude.

I also appreciate the work of photographer Kevin Brett. His expertise and creativity have richly enhanced the project.

To countless other students and friends who encouraged and sustained me throughout the project, I give thanks.

INTRODUCTION

Reverse glass painting involves creating a mirror image of a picture on a piece of glass, foreground first and background last, so that the image can be viewed correctly on the opposite side of the glass. In early nineteenth-century America, the technique was often used to make panels to decorate clock doors and the tops of looking glasses (the historic term for mirrors).

I have been involved with studying and teaching reverse glass painting since 1977, when I attended a seminar on the subject taught by Peg Emery, a noted painter and author. It was love at first brush stroke, and it continues to be my favorite Early American decorative technique.

I am now an accredited teacher of reverse glass painting for the Historical Society of Early American Decoration (HSEAD), a national society dedicated to the research and education of several Early American decorative techniques. I am working on a video on reverse glass painting, as part of HSEAD's Master Teaching

Above: Landscape with a gold leaf border by Anne Dimock. This design was originally in an architectural looking glass.

Series of Early American Decorative Arts. I teach at home year-round and have taught seminars at the Farmers Museum in Cooperstown, New York; Historic Eastfield in Nassau, New York; the Isabel O'Neil studio in New York City; and in several studios of HSEAD members. I have taught several workshops at HSEAD's national meeting. I also do reproduction work, including one glass that was sold at Sotheby's!

In this book I will share tips and techniques for you to develop your skills in reverse glass painting. There are fourteen projects to work on, arranged in order of difficulty. Some of the designs are from original pieces or adapted from originals, and a few are my own designs adapted from pieces done in other mediums. Enjoy!

Left: *Empire looking glass by Anne Dimock with a primitive fruit design.* Below: *Author Anne Dimock in her studio.*

A Brief History of Reverse Glass Painting

The art of painting on the back side of glass is an ancient technique. The earliest known surviving example is the *Paris Plate*, done around 200 A.D. It depicts the mythological theme of the Judgment of Paris and can be seen at the Corning Museum of Glass in Corning, New York.

Gold leafing, a popular method in Europe of overlaying objects with a thin sheet of gold, was used extensively to decorate glass objects from 300 A.D. to 1100 A.D. Also in medieval Europe, artists began painting reverse-glass pictures with religious themes.

By the mid-1700s, a process had been developed to transfer ink from paper to glass. The transferred lines were then back-painted by an artist. In 1760, John Baptiste Glomie revived the early medieval gold leaf technique on glass. The process was named *verre eglomise* in his honor, and it is a name still associated with gold leaf designs on glass.

In early America, circa 1780–1820, reverse glass was seen on insets in fine Hepplewhite and Sheraton furniture. Eglomise panels were seen in Hepplewhite and Sheraton looking glasses, as were some painted designs.

Above: *Gold and silver leaf Basket of Roses by Anne Dimock.*

Empire looking glass with ebonized and gilded columns, featuring a picture of a sailing ship with an elaborate stenciled border.

Sheration or "tabernacle" looking glass picturing a lovely mourning scene with a gold leaf border.

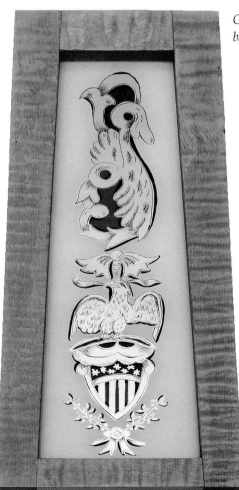

Gold leaf and painted tablet showing a naval battle (above) and throat for a banjo clock (left).

Portraits of George Washington were common. In the years between 1800 and 1860, reverse-glass panels were used to decorate looking glasses and tablets in clocks. Empire-style panels for mirrors usually had borders of gold leaf, fine stencil designs, or both, with painted landscapes, fruit, and naval scenes. Folk art looking glasses had simpler designs without borders or were outlined with primitive dots.

Tablets were made for a variety of clock styles, including shelf, banjo, and pillar and scroll. Early clock tablets had beautifully executed gold leaf and fine stenciled borders. Many had very detailed painted designs where outlines were done with a pen. Some had one-piece, stenciled designs which were back painted, or had frosted glass tablets that imitated etched glass. By the 1860s, a technique called *decalcomania* became popular in America. Special prints, or transfers, were adhered to glass, and then back painted to add color. Tinsel painting also emerged in the mid-1800s. These glasses had dark outlines, transparent colors on the design elements, and an opaque background. Tinfoil was then placed behind the transparent design.

In the twentieth century, reverse glass painting fell out of vogue. Many of the beautiful glass panels were lost over time due to paint deterioration or breakage. In recent years, however, members of the Historical Society of Early American Decoration and other groups have revived the technique by making faithful reproductions of the old designs. Other painters have taken a personal approach to the old art, creating their own designs.

Top: *A miniature ogee clock tablet showing the black linework applied by decal and the back-painted colors.* Bottom: *The reverse side demonstrates the effect obtained from back-painted linework.*

Tools and Materials

This chapter introduces the tools and materials you will need to make your own reverse glass paintings. Most of these supplies can be found at local hardware or arts and crafts stores. If you are unable to find something, refer to the Supplies and Resources section at the back of the book.

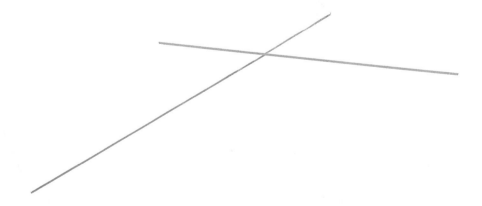

GLASS

In reverse glass painting, the picture is painted directly on the glass surface, so it is important to get good quality glass. Single-pane window glass from a hardware store or glass shop works well. Check to make sure there are no scratches on the surface or nicks on the edges. Thin old glass is especially nice for gold leaf designs. Bubbles and waviness add interest and beauty to your paintings.

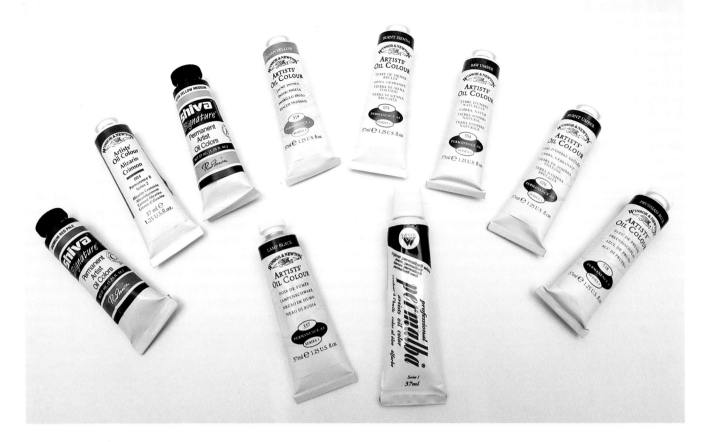

PAINTS

In this book, we will use oil paints. I have found that certain brands work best for me. For cadmium red pale and yellow medium, I use the Shiva brand. For white, I prefer Weber Permalba. The rest of the paints I recommend are Winsor Newton Artists' Oils. Colors include Prussian blue, alizarin crimson, burnt umber, raw umber, Indian yellow, burnt sienna, Venetian red, and lamp black.

BRUSHES

Use the following Loew-Cornell brushes: the #7050-10/0 script liner, for fine line work; the #7400-1/8-inch angled shader, to clean up errors; and the #410-1/4-inch stippler, for stippling trees and borders. You will also need two of each of the following Scharff brushes: the #150, sizes 2, 4, and 10. Also from Scharff, purchase two of the #550-1/2-inch and one of the #550-3/4-inch brushes. Finally, get the Mack XCaliber 4/0 sword striper.

QUICK DRY GILDING SIZE

Size is used as a medium to mix with the paints. The brands I suggest are Rolco or Luco. To keep the size fresh, punch a hole in the bottom of the can near the edge with a roofing nail. Remove the nail to extract size and replace when not using.

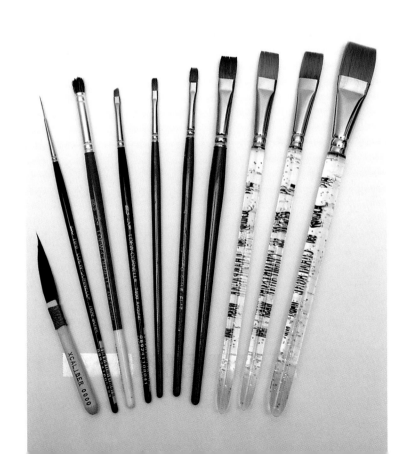

RAPIDOGRAPH PENS AND BLACK INK

You will need a size 3/0 pen, for line work and tracings, and a size 0, 1, or 2, for dots on dot-to-dot designs. Black Rapidograph ink #3080-F can be purchased where you find the pens.

BRIDGE

An artist's bridge, made from an inflexible piece of wood or plastic with 3/4-inch to 1-inch blocks under each end, is used to keep your hand steady and out of the wet paint.

SMALL CAPS

Use small bottle caps or plastic communion cups to hold the mixed paints while you work.

PALETTE KNIVES

Purchase two or three 3-inch trowel blade knives for mixing your paints.

PALETTE PAPER

Acrylic-coated 9 x 12-inch palette paper is used for mixing paints. Do not use any paper that is wax coated. Freezer paper also works. Use the shiny side for mixing the paints.

MINERAL SPIRITS

For cleaning brushes, buy mineral spirits in a quart or gallon size. I do not recommend odorless mineral spirits, because it does not effectively remove the painting medium from the brushes.

PINK SOAP

After you are done painting for the day and have washed your brushes with mineral spirits, clean them with Pink Soap until no more color comes out. Then rinse the brushes with hot water and shape them. Be sure the brushes are dry before using them again.

LIGHTER FLUID

Lighter fluid is used to clean up errors made while painting. Ronsonol brand is more highly refined and does not leave an oily film.

ABRASIVE CLEANSER

The glass you paint on must be clean. Bon Ami or Bar Keepers Friend cleansers are gentle enough not to scratch the glass.

SANDPAPER

Use a small piece of 100- or 150-grit sandpaper or a carborundum stone to dull the edges of your glass. Smooth out any small nicks to lessen the possibility of future stress fractures.

TRACING PAPER

Tracing paper is used to trace patterns, and is also used between the pattern and the glass to deflect double images. Get the most transparent kind available.

CARDBOARD

This is used as a mounting board for the tracing and glass. Use any old piece that is available.

TEMPLATES

Circle and oval templates are needed for tracing and gold leaf etching.

SOFT RAGS OR PAPER TOWELS

These are used for cleaning up. Cut old t-shirts or cotton knit fabric into squares about 6 inches. Cut good-quality paper towels into quarters and have them handy at your work table. The smaller pieces cause less waste and better-quality paper towels make less lint.

MASKING TAPE

Use regular masking tape for mounting the pattern and glass to the cardboard. Do not use painters tape.

TACK CLOTH

Use tack cloth to remove dust from the work surface, the palette paper, and the glass.

   Once the package is opened, store the tack cloth in an airtight container, such as a baby food jar.

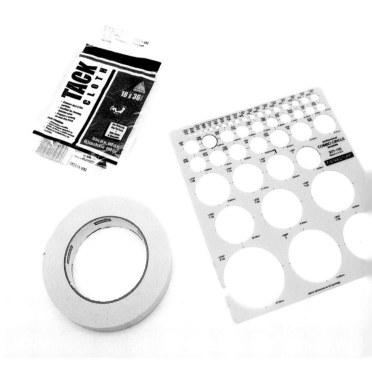

GOLD LEAF

Gold leaf is often used to decorate borders on glass paintings as well as beautiful scenic designs. Use 23-carat glass gold leaf. I use the Monarch brand.

GELATIN AND DISTILLED WATER FOR GELATIN SIZE

Gelatin is available in sheets. The sheets are added to distilled water and boiled to make gelatin size, which is used to adhere gold leaf to glass. To make the size, see page 41.

PYREX CARAFE

You need a small container in which to heat your size. I use a small Pyrex carafe.

HOT PLATE

Buy a hot plate to keep at your work space for heating the size, rather than getting up to use the stove in the kitchen.

SOFT BRUSH

A soft 1-inch brush is used to apply the size to the glass.

CHINA MARKER

To mark the glass for placement of the gold leaf, use a china marker.

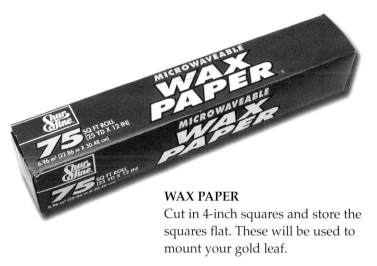

WAX PAPER

Cut in 4-inch squares and store the squares flat. These will be used to mount your gold leaf.

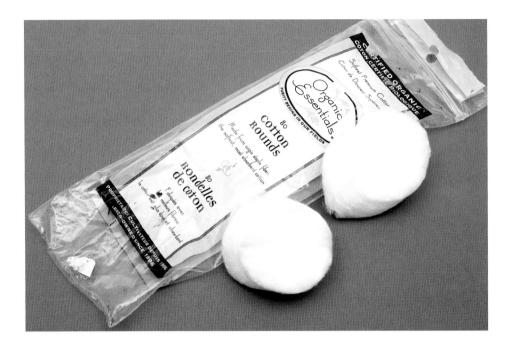

COSMETIC PADS

You will need pure cotton pads
for burnishing the gold.

GRAPHITE PAPER

Transfer your design to the gold leaf with graphite
paper. Be sure to use real graphite paper
and not a substitute.

STYLUS

Use a stylus with the graphite
paper to trace the design onto
the gold leaf.

CRAFT KNIFE
To etch the gold leaf, use a craft knife with a #16 blade.

BLACK PAPER
Place black paper under the glass when you etch or stencil to make it easier to see what you are doing.

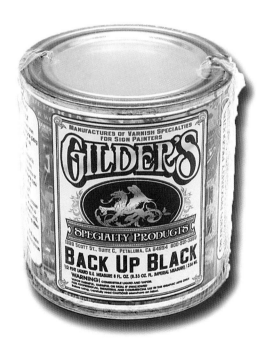

BACK UP BLACK
Apply this product to back up the gold leaf once the etching is complete.

AMMONIA AND WHITING
The excess gold is removed with ammonia and cotton pads. Whiting can also be used with the ammonia to help remove excess gold.

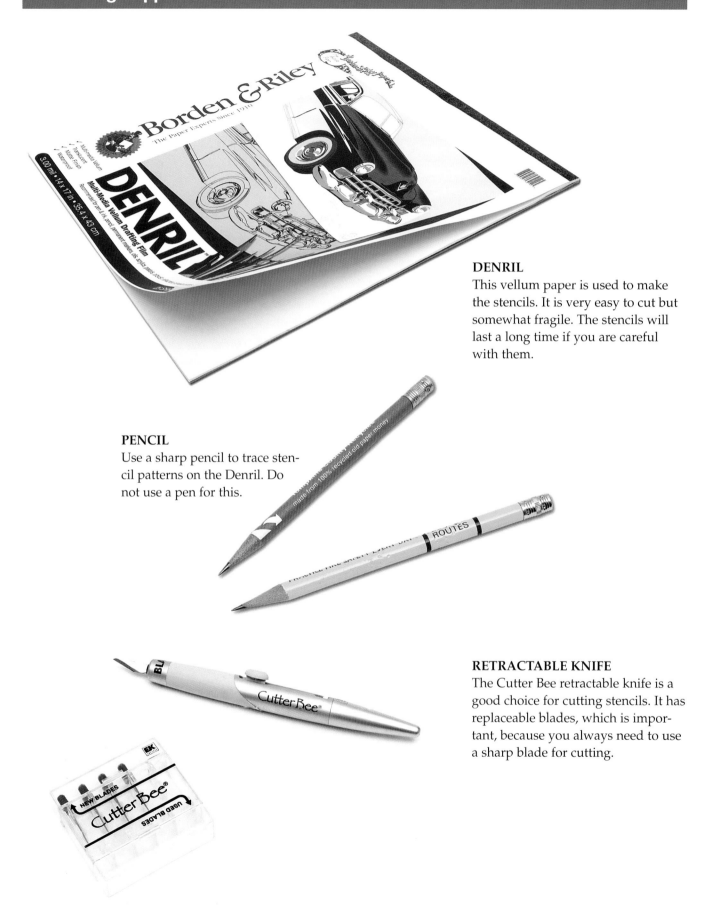

DENRIL

This vellum paper is used to make the stencils. It is very easy to cut but somewhat fragile. The stencils will last a long time if you are careful with them.

PENCIL

Use a sharp pencil to trace stencil patterns on the Denril. Do not use a pen for this.

RETRACTABLE KNIFE

The Cutter Bee retractable knife is a good choice for cutting stencils. It has replaceable blades, which is important, because you always need to use a sharp blade for cutting.

GLASS WITH BLACK BACKING

Tape a piece of black cardboard to an 8 x 10-inch piece of glass to use as the surface to cut the stencils on. The black behind the glass will make it easier for you to see what you are cutting.

BRONZE LINING POWDERS

Lining powders are used to execute the stencil design. Rich pale gold and aluminum (silver) are needed for the designs in this book.

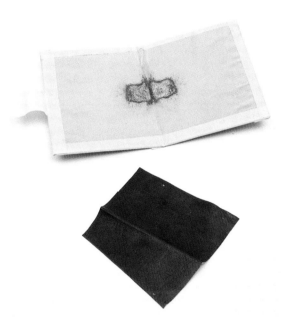

APPLICATOR

Fine doeskin or Ultrasuede facile cut in 3-inch or 4-inch squares is used for applying the powders.

VARNISH BRUSH

To apply the varnish, use a good-quality 1-inch foam brush or a top-quality 1-inch varnish brush (very soft bristles).

VARNISH

Tung oil varnish, with 55 percent tung oil, is used for stenciling. Waterlox Original Marine Finish Gloss and McCloskey Man O'War Gloss are two brands that work well.

ONE SHOT PAINTS

These are used to back up stenciled borders. Colors used in this book are fire red, black, chrome yellow, medium green, reflex blue, dark brown, and white.

Basic Skills

In this chapter, you will become familiar with the skills needed for creating your own reverse glass paintings. Familiarize yourself with these techniques and refer to this section as you work on the projects in this book.

Choose a piece of glass that is the appropriate size for the design. It is very important to take extra care in the preparation of the glass since this is the surface you will be painting on.

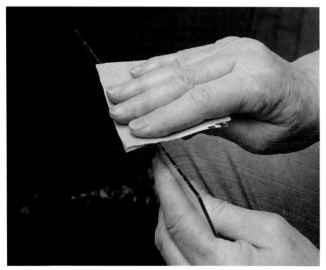

Sand the edges of the glass with a piece of sandpaper or carborundum stone. Be careful not to touch the flat surface of the glass with the sandpaper, as it will leave scratches. Smooth any small nicks on the edges. Sanding reduces the possibility of stress fractures when framing and dulls the edges so you won't cut yourself when painting.

Using a cotton rag and abrasive cleanser with water, thoroughly scrub the glass on both sides.

Rinse the glass with hot water and then wipe it dry with a paper towel. Make sure there is no cloudiness or streaking. If there is, scrub it again. Once it is clean and dry, handle it by the edges to avoid getting fingerprints on the surface of the glass.

Before You Start Painting

- Reverse glass painting is so named because the image is executed on the reverse of the side it is viewed. When you place your tracing on the cardboard, the picture will be a reversal of the finished design. You will paint it in reverse order, from the very finest details first to the background last. This takes some getting used to, but it is worth all the effort.
- Have an idea of how you plan to frame the finished panel. Make sure the glass fits your frame before you start painting.
- If you have an antique clock or looking glass, it would be wise to research the correct design for the period of your piece.

Trace on tracing paper or photocopy the desired pattern. Then cut a piece of cardboard about 3 inches larger than the glass.

Tape the pattern to the cardboard, leaving more space at the top. Your tracing is a reversal of what will be the finished picture. Place two 4-inch pieces of tape on the cardboard centered at the top corners.

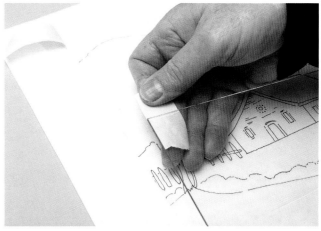

With two 3-inch pieces of tape, make tabs for the top corners of the glass: Fold one-third of the tape on the middle one-third of itself, and then fasten the remaining one-third of the tape to the front side of the glass.

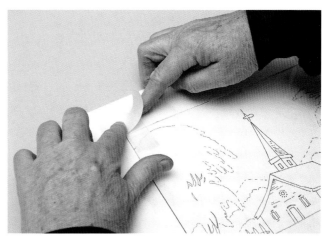

Place the glass, with tabs down, over the pattern on the cardboard and fasten it with masking tape over the tabs.

Slide a piece of tracing paper in between the pattern and the glass. The tracing paper keeps you from seeing double images as you do the line work.

Before you start painting, mix the colors you'll be using. On the palette paper, squeeze out as much paint as needed of the main color—usually the lightest one—and small amounts of toning colors.

Add the darker colors to the light colors, a little at a time and mixing well with the palette knife, until you get the desired shade. For example, when mixing green, the main color will be Shiva yellow and the toning colors Prussian blue and cadmium red pale. Add blue to yellow first, in small amounts.

When the green is a close match to the design, add cadmium red pale to soften the color.

Order of Painting

1. Line work. Do all the line work first; then allow the glass to dry for twenty-four hours.
2. Glazes. Execute glazes in all the areas indicated and then let the glass dry for twenty-four hours.
3. Small areas. Paint all small areas, such as windows, doors, flowers, flags, and so on, making sure not to paint two adjoining areas on the same day. These areas may be solid or blended. Pay close attention to painting foreground areas first.
4. Stippling. All the greens and yellows on trees should be executed at this point, as these colors tend to blend a bit. Border stippling needs to be done one color at a time with twenty-four hours drying time in between. If there is umber stippling on the trees, you can do this stippling at the same time you do your line work; it needs time to dry before green is added.
5. Medium areas. The larger areas, such as houses, boats, clothing, fruit, and so on, are painted after the smaller areas are dry. It may take you more than one day to complete all these areas.
6. Backgrounds. Usually, the grassy areas on a landscape design are painted first and need to dry for twenty-four hours before you execute sky and water.

When you get the color to the desired shade, add quick size to the paint.

Blend until the mixture is about half paint and half size. It should drop easily from the palette knife.

Scoop the mixture into a soda cap or plastic communion cup to keep the paint viable while you work.

Testing Your Color Mixture

For the projects in this book or other designs you want to match, you should test to see if you have the correct color by putting a small amount of your paint mixture on a piece of scrap glass. Look at it through the glass and compare it to the color photo in this book or the design you are copying. If the color is too dark, start over, as it takes too much light color to get the mixture back to the desired shade. Old glass will often have a greenish tint which will affect the paint color you mix.

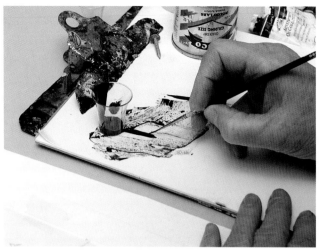

Now you are ready to paint the lines. Squeeze about ¹/₂ inch of burnt umber paint on the palette paper, and then mix in a tiny bit of lamp black. Add size, blend well, and put the mixture into a cap. Take the 10/0 script liner and dip it into the paint, working it through all the bristles on the palette paper. This is called dressing the brush. When the brush is fully loaded, roll the brush handle in your fingers to bring the bristles to a point.

On the prepared glass, paint all the line work shown on the tracing. You need to check the color photograph or the original you are copying to see which lines are painted. For example, in this photo you would not paint the lines indicating the mountains. Keep the brush perpendicular to the glass, resting your hand on a bridge or the back of your other hand. Only the tips of the bristles should touch the glass. Dress the brush as often as necessary. Move to a new spot on the palette paper when dressing the brush to avoid working in sticky paint. If the brush starts dragging, rinse it in mineral spirits and wipe it dry, then reload.

If you find you've made a line crooked or too wide, you can remove it. First place a small amount of lighter fluid in a cap. Take the ¹/₈-inch angled shader, dip it in the lighter fluid, and wipe off the excess on a paper towel. Now brush over the unwanted line to clean it off. You may need to rinse the shader in the lighter fluid, dry it, and brush again to remove all the undesirable paint. Don't worry if the lines are a bit uneven in color or width; this adds to the character of the piece. For black lines, mix lamp black paint with size. Once you've completed the line work, remove the glass from the pattern.

Thin line work can be done in pen, particularly on glass tablets for clocks. To execute these lines, use a Rapidograph pen with a 3/0 or 4/0 (.25 or .18) point, depending on the width of the desired line work.

Fill the pen with the ink specially made for these pens, following the directions that come with the pen.

With the glass set up on your pattern, complete all the line work, making sure the pen is always perpendicular to the glass. If you have it at an angle, you can ruin the pen. If the ink stops flowing, shake the pen gently side to side until you hear a clicking sound, then proceed. Check to make sure the pen is not out of ink. Clean off any errors with water. After you've completed the pen work, take the ink out of the pen and rinse the nib, so that the ink doesn't dry in it. These pens can be difficult, so treat them carefully.

Dot Designs

Dot designs are also executed with a pen. Use a #0, #1, or #2 (.35 or .60) point, depending on the size of the dots you desire.

Holding the pen perpendicular to the glass, touch the point down and pick it up in succession to make dots following the line on the pattern. Again, these are primitive designs, so it is not necessary to keep the dots all the same size or distance apart. When you complete your dot work, take the ink out of the pen and rinse the nib out.

Stippling, or gently bouncing your brush, creates images in negative space, such as the trees and bushes, allowing the background colors you will apply later, such as the blue for the sky, to show through. Stippling is also used on the decorative borders of many glass designs.

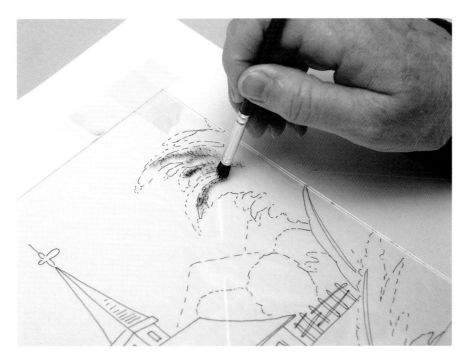

When stippling, mix the color paint and put it in a cap. Use the ¹/₄-inch deerfoot stippler; dip it into the paint, and then wipe most of it out of the brush onto the palette. Pounce the brush gently on the palette to see if you have enough of the paint out. You want to make dots, not blobs, on the glass.

Pounce the stippler gently in the areas shown on the tracing, following the original piece or the color photograph, actually touching the glass with the side of the brush with the longer bristles. To reload the brush, pick up a bit of paint from the palette. Only a small amount is needed. Remember, the stippling should not be solid.

Occasionally, you will see where a design has been created in the stippling by pulling a dry brush through. Stipple the area in question, then dip the $\frac{1}{8}$-inch angled shader into the lighter fluid, wipe dry on a paper towel, and draw through the stippling to create the desired design. Rinse the brush, then dry and repeat for entire design.

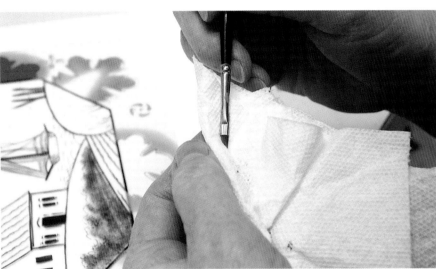

Shadows in old reverse glass designs were created using a transparent glaze of color, usually burnt umber. Blend about $1/4$ inch of burnt umber. Use a ratio of $2/3$ to $3/4$ size to $1/4$ paint, depending on the transparency of the glaze. Test on glass. Mix the glaze well and put it in a cap. Use one of the Scharff 150 brushes; the size of brush used will depend on the area to be glazed. Dip the brush in the paint and dress it out on the palette, stroking back and forth to fully load the bristles. Stroke evenly over the area to be glazed, using a light touch to avoid making ridges. Try not to overwork these areas. Then let the paint settle. Wait twenty-four hours before continuing.

Some glazes are achieved by a method called side loading.

Start by putting a small amount of the desired color paint on the palette. Then put a bit of size in a cap. Taking an appropriate Scharff brush, dip it in the size and dress it out on the palette. Draw one side of the brush into the paint and dress it back and forth until it creates shadings from dark to light color.

Now go to the glass and paint the area desired with a single smooth stroke. Let it settle for a minute; if it is too streaky, redo it. Reload the brush often. If you are making many side-loaded strokes, you may need to clean the brush and move the paint to a new spot on the palette.

Blending two colors together on the glass is another way to create dimension in the design. This technique takes a bit of practice, so try it a few times on a scrap piece of glass first.

Mix the colors to be used in the blended area, following directions for mixing paint on page 28. Put each color in a cap. For smaller areas of blending, such as fruit and leaves, use Scharff #2 and #4 brushes, one for each color. For larger areas, such as water, grass, and sky, use Scharff 150 #10 and Scharff 550 ¹/₂-inch and ³/₄-inch brushes, one for each color. Choose the brushes according to the size of the area to be painted. Have everything ready before starting, as it is necessary to work quickly. Then decide where to start. On water, grasses, and sky, start at the top and work down. On smaller areas, it will depend on where the colors are on the unit.

Pick up the first color with an appropriate size brush and dress the brush on the palette. Paint the area that calls for that color.

Repeat with the second color. Always maintain a light touch with the brush, because pressing too hard will make streaks and actually remove some of the paint.

Use the lighter color brush to gently pull the two colors together.

Hold the glass up from time to time so you can see the front as you blend on the back. Remember, the appearance on the front is what matters. When checking your blending, hold the glass over a dark surface so light will not shine through and distort the painting.

When you have achieved the desired blend as viewed from the front of the glass, move on to the next color. Caution: the paint starts drying right away, so work as quickly as possible to avoid harsh lines.

Making Clouds

Paint the blue sky.

Quickly pick up a bit of white on your finger.

Hold the glass so that you can see the front; push the white through the blue with your finger until you create the cloud you want. You may need to wipe your finger off and repeat the process a few times.

Making Skies and Mountains

Skies on glass are generally two or three colors, starting with blue at the top, and then fading to yellow and then to pink. Blend the blue and yellow and the yellow and pink if applicable, bringing the last color all the way to the horizon. Now pick up the mountain color, in this case the blue sky color, on a #10 or ½-inch brush. Hold the glass so that you can see the front, and pull the brush up one side down the other, very deliberately, to make the mountain. You may have to make a second pass to complete the bottom part of the mountain. Every mountain is going to be a little different and that's all right. Don't overwork them.

Stippling Bushes and Trees

To add trees and bushes that have a subtle effect, you can stipple them through the sky color. After blending the entire sky, take the stippling brush with the appropriate color, hold the glass so that you can see the front, and stipple the trees. Don't overdo this by pressing too hard with the stippler.

Making a Sky-to-Water Horizon

To make the horizon where sky meets water, paint the sky first, then paint the water.

To create the horizon line, pull the water brush carefully along the edge of the sky, just barely blending the two.

While you're painting, you will want to change colors frequently and will need to clean your brushes with mineral spirits.

First wipe out the paint on a paper towel, squeezing the bristles between your fingers.

Have a small container of mineral spirits at your workspace. Quickly dip the brush in the mineral spirits.

Squeeze the brush out on a paper towel. Continue this sequence until most of the paint is out of the brush. Gently swish the brush in the mineral spirits one more time and squeeze it out again. The brush is now ready to use with another color.

When done painting for the day, clean the brush as described above. Then dip the brush in Pink Soap, working it through the bristles with your fingers.

For thicker brushes, use the palm of your hand. Squeeze out the soap and repeat until the color is gone.

Rinse the soap out with hot water and shape the brush before putting it away.

When doing gold leaf work, it is especially important that the glass is extremely clean before you start. Any impurities will cause the gold leaf to look cloudy. Place tabs on the upper corners on the front of the glass as previously described on page 27.

Place the tracing of the design on the table facing the direction of the finished picture. Lay the glass on top with the tab side up. This is opposite from when you are painting lines.

Take a china marker and draw lines around the area to be gold leafed, leaving an extra $1/4$ inch on all sides.

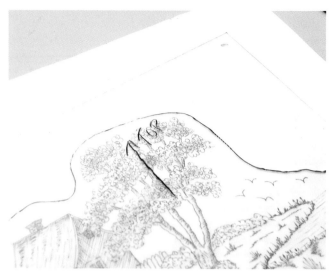

Draw an arrow pointing to the top of the glass with the marker. Write TOP or NO on the glass so you don't make the mistake of putting gold on this side of the glass.

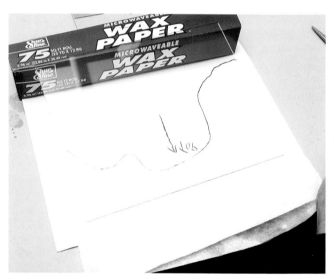

In the next stage, you will be using liquid, so you will want to prop the glass up on a box or bridge, marked side down, putting it on a slant to allow the liquid to run off. The arrow should be pointing down.

Now, you will make the gelatin size that will adhere the gold leaf to the glass. Put two diamonds of gelatin and one cup of distilled water in a small, clean carafe. Place the carafe on a burner and heat slowly to a boil, swirling the water around a few times so the gelatin doesn't stick to the bottom. Once the gelatin is dissolved and the water boils, turn the temperature down so that the water is just simmering.

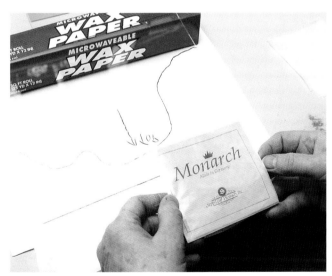

Slide the gold leaf out of the cellophane packet carefully. The leaf is fragile and sticks to everything it touches. Have 4-inch squares of wax paper ready. Open the book of leaf to the first sheet of gold slowly and carefully, being sure not to touch it. Make sure there is a minimum of air movement; it will cause the gold leaf to crumple up or blow away.

Lay a square of wax paper on the gold.

Shut the book and rub gently across it with your hand.

Reopen the book and remove the sheet of wax paper with the gold now mounted on it. Mount enough sheets to do one coat of gold on your glass.

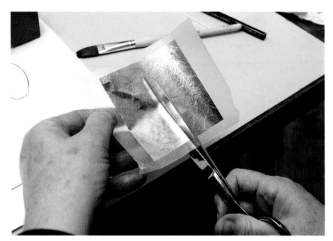

For borders or small areas, cut the mounted sheets of gold into appropriate size pieces. To make sure the scissors don't stick to the gold, wipe the blades of your scissors with one of the rouge sheets from the book of gold leaf before cutting the gold.

Now that the glass, size, and gold leaf are ready, you can start. Dip a soft 1-inch brush in the hot size.

Go to the upper left-hand corner of the tilted glass, and spread the size over the glass, covering enough area to lay your first sheet of gold.

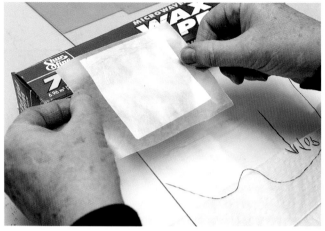

Quickly pick up a mounted piece of gold leaf and lay the gold side on the wet glass. Carefully remove the wax paper.

Now put more size to the right of the first piece and lay the next piece. Continue covering the entire area that is marked out, finishing the top row first. Let the glass dry for two hours or until all the gold is shiny.

After the glass dries, take a cotton pad and gently brush off any loose gold.

Then burnish the gold with your cotton pad, rubbing the entire surface to make it shiny. You need to rub harder to soften the edges, especially along seam lines and in any holes. If you don't soften seams on the first coat, they will show later. Remove loose gold from the cotton often, as it will scratch the gold on the glass. It may not look great when you get done, but the second coat will cover this. Be careful not to scratch the gold with fingernails or jewelry.

Reheat the size. Place the glass back on the stand, this time with the arrow pointing up. Mount more gold leaf. Start at the top left of the gold area, apply size, and then place the gold. Continue across the top and then down the glass. Let it dry again for at least an hour.

Use a piece of cotton and brush off any excess. Do not burnish at this point. If there are any holes still showing, lay small patches with hot size and small pieces of gold.

Once the gold is solid on the glass in the area where the design will be placed, fasten the tracing in the top two corners over the gold, making sure the pattern is now a reversal of the finished design.

Slide a piece of graphite paper between the glass and the tracing.

Gold Leaf Tips

- Trace the pattern on tracing paper. Do not use a photocopy. It is good practice to trace just the outlines on the tracing paper, and then take a pencil and sketch in the shading. This will give you a feel for etching, using the pencil like an etcher.
- Etch as soon as possible after applying the gold leaf to the glass. You have about a week before the gold becomes harder and thus more difficult to remove.

Place a piece of black cardboard under the glass. Since the gold acts as a mirror, adjust the light so there isn't any glare on your gold. Use a craft knife with a #16 blade for the etching. The blade needs to be dull, not a sharp point, so it may need to be dulled on a piece of sandpaper.

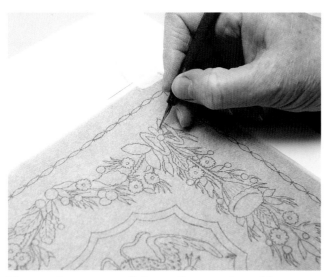

Use a stylus to trace all the outlines on the gold.

Find a place on the gold where there is no design and practice etching. Hold the knife like a pencil and keep the point of the blade flat against the glass. Most etching lines have some curve to them, so think about that as you practice. The lines you create need to be seen from a distance. You may need to dull the knife more if your lines are too thin.

Remove the tracing and graphite paper. It is now ready to etch.

Once you get a feel for how the knife works, start on the design. Do all the outlines first, then go back and start shading. When shading, start light; you can always go back and do more.

When you outline trees, make curlicues, not lines. Do not etch water lines, birds, stripes, and some other details. These details are indicated in red on the patterns.

Be sure the black cardboard is always under the glass. Put a tissue under your hand if you have to lay it on the gold to avoid scratching it. Stop etching every once in a while and look at the piece from a few feet away to be sure the etching can be seen.

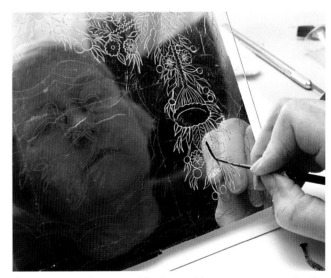

Once you are happy with the etching, you can apply the Back Up Black. Put a small amount in a cap. Use an appropriate size brush and paint over all the etched areas, just covering the outside etching line. Hold the glass up at an angle so light shows through the front and so you can see if you have covered all of the lines. Keep checking as you work.

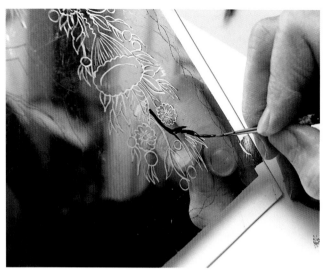

For smaller areas, switch to a 10/0 brush. The Back Up Black is thick, so you may need to put a tiny bit of mineral spirits on the brush to soften it. Do this only if necessary. After you cover all the etched areas, use the 10/0 brush to paint the water lines, stripes, and birds, following the tracing lines. Paint directly on the gold. If necessary, rinse out the brush in mineral spirits and dry, and then continue. For complicated designs that take a while to back up, it may be necessary to throw away the black and get another small amount out of the can. Let the black dry for about an hour.

Now put a small amount of ammonia in a cap. Using a cotton pad, soak up some ammonia.

Gently scrub off the gold that isn't backed.

If the gold hasn't been on the glass for too many days, it should come right off without too much work. If the gold isn't coming off easily, use a little bit of whiting with the ammonia. This is a gentle abrasive, so be more careful as you scrub.

When washing back over water lines, go with the lines, not across them. Dry the glass frequently. When the excess gold is gone, carefully clean the glass with water and dry.

First, use a pencil to trace the stencil design on a piece of Denril that is 2 inches larger than the design on all sides. The lines traced will determine where to cut, so a bad tracing will produce a bad stencil.

Place the Denril on the glass with black paper underneath. Using a retractable knife, cut the stencil out. Press only hard enough on the knife to cut through the Denril or you will dull your knife. Cut right on the pencil line. It may be helpful to use a magnifying lens to do the cutting. I find it helpful when cutting curves to use the hand that is holding the stencil to turn the stencil while holding the knife still.

Try to always cut while pulling the knife toward you, as you have better control. Cutting takes a little practice so trace some extras. If an error is made while cutting, use that piece as practice and cut out another.

Most stencils are referred to as positive stencils, where the powders are applied through the opening in the Denril. A negative stencil is a solid piece of Denril that the powders are applied around.

Stenciling on reverse glass is usually used for border designs. Before you can execute the border, however, you need a stripe. Set up the glass with the pattern.

Most stripes are black. Mix $1/4$ inch of lamp black with size and put it in a cap. Dip the XCaliber striper in the paint and dress the brush on the palette. Make sure the bristles are full of paint.

Now, hold the brush with the tapered side down. Using your pinkie finger along the edge of the glass as a guide, put down the tip of brush ahead of where the stripe starts. Establish the width desired by how much pressure is applied to the brush. Now pull the brush down the glass slowly, holding your hand steady. Don't drop your hand down as it gets toward the end of the stripe, as it will make the stripe wider.

Repeat for remaining stripes.

Use the $1/8$-inch angled shader and lighter fluid to remove extra paint at the corners.

When making a round or oval stripe, twist the brush gently in your fingers to help the bristles follow around the curve more easily. It will be necessary to stop and reposition the brush often in this case. Let it dry for twenty-four hours.

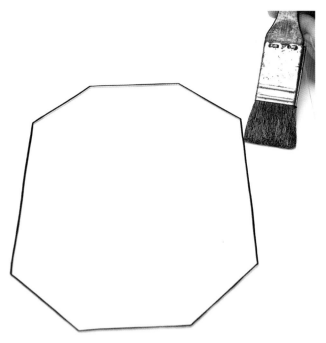

Use a 1-inch sponge or fine varnish brush to varnish just halfway across the stripe. Don't skimp with the varnish, but don't flood the glass either. Check carefully for any skips before you set it aside to dry.

With the glass on the pattern, start with one corner unit, placing the cut stencil on the tacky varnish where indicated on the pattern.

Slide black cardboard underneath the glass.

You will be using bronze lining powders to stencil the borders. I like to have my powders in separate packets. Cut a piece of velveteen or short-napped, no-ridge corduroy about 3 x 6 inches. Tape the edges to a piece of sturdy cardboard, nap side out. Fold it in half, cloth side in. You may want to cut the cardboard at the fold. Make two of these. Now put about ¼ teaspoon of powder in the center of each packet, one for rich pale gold and one for silver. You will also need two pieces of doeskin or ultra suede facile, one for each color.

About two hours after you varnish the glass, start checking the tackiness of the varnish. Touch a corner of the varnish with a piece of Denril. It should not stick to the varnish; it should make just a little click. At that point it is ready to stencil.

Take a doeskin square and fold it in half over the top part of your finger.

Fold the loose doeskin back against the top of your finger and hold it there with your middle finger.

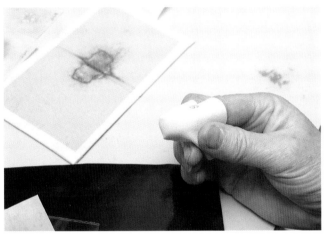

A section will be stretched tightly over the end of your finger.

Pick up a small bit of appropriate color powder on the tight area on the end of your finger. Tap it off on the cloth.

Go to your stencil on the glass and pat a very small amount of powder through the stencil. Pick up a bit more powder and start on the edge of the stencil. Begin to polish the powder into the varnish. If the unit is solidly gold or silver, polish the entire stencil area.

If the unit is shaded, polish the edges brightly.

Then shade off toward the center to create a gradual shading with very little or no powder right at the center.

Be sure the unit is polished brightly where it touches the stripe.

After forty-eight hours, take a cotton knit rag and distilled water and clean the stenciled area.

With negative stencils, you shade away from the stencil. Polish brightly all around the stencil, then shade off uniformly. Using a clean area on your doeskin, pick up any excess powder before you remove your stencil. Move on to the other corners and repeat.

Repeat with all other stencil units, changing finger doeskin for each color. Let stenciled glass dry for forty-eight hours. Clean the Denril stencils with paper towels and lighter fluid.

You will pick up loose powders, so switch to a clean part of your rag. Dry the area carefully with another rag. Let the glass stand to dry for an hour, then varnish the border right over the stencils, just on the border. Wait forty-eight hours and apply a second coat of varnish, just on the border. Wait another twenty-four hours before backing the border with One Shot.

Often shaded corner units have red or green behind them. You want to use One Shot enamels for backing all stencils, as they won't bleed through the varnish. For a positive stencil, paint the One Shot behind the whole unit, being careful not to go over the edge.

For a negative stencil, fill in the center and go just over the edge of the stenciling.

Small flower units often have a circle of color painted behind the flower. Before you paint these, use a template and mark circles on the front of the glass with a Sharpie.

The circles serve as a guide to paint the units on the varnished side.

After twenty-four hours, you can paint the background. Use One Shot color behind the entire border.

When framing reverse glass paintings, it is important that the painted side doesn't have anything laying against it. Use small wooden strips to hold the glass in the frame.

Glue the wooden strips to the side of the rabbet but not to the glass. Use four strips for the top, bottom, and sides. You can now put a paper dust cover on the back of the frame.

Primitive Houses with Trees

Your first project is a simple country landscape taken from an antique design done around 1850. It will take you about a week to complete and will help you develop the basics to master the craft, as well as some special techniques, such as making clouds.

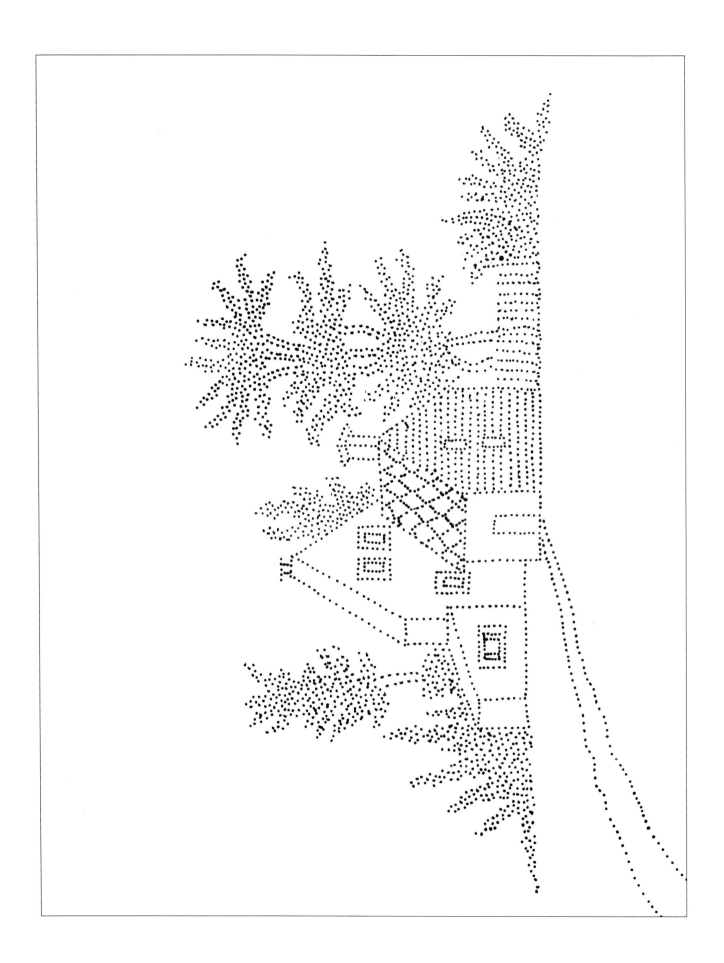

This project, like those that follow, will take several days to complete because of the time needed for drying between steps. Allow the painting to dry for a full twenty-four hours after each day's work. Prepare a 7 x 9-inch piece of glass and then set up the pattern (see pages 26–27).

Use a size 2 Rapidograph pen and follow the pattern to put all the black dots on the glass. Hold the pen vertical at all times. It is not necessary to have the same number of dots as the pattern. The ink dries very fast but be careful not to smear it as you're working. If you make a mistake, it can be removed easily with a damp paper towel.

Now mix ¹/₄ inch of burnt umber with size for a glaze (see page 34). Using a #2 brush, apply brown glazes on the house and tree trunks in the areas indicated on the photo of the finished piece.

Mix ¹/₄ inch white with a small amount of Shiva yellow and burnt umber to match the picture and add size. Using a #2 brush, paint the fence and path.

At this point, the picture should look like this from the side you're painting on.

If you hold the glass up and look at it from the front, or the reverse side from which you are painting, the picture should look like this.

Mix ¼ inch of cadmium red with size and paint the roofs of the houses.

The front of the picture should look like this.

Mix ¼ inch of white with size. Use a #2 brush to paint the taller house and the lean-to, covering the glazes you previously painted in these areas.

Then add a tiny bit of Shiva yellow to the white and paint over the dots on the end of the smaller house.

Mix ½ inch of Shiva yellow with Prussian blue, adding a little bit at a time so it doesn't get too blue. Then add a little cadmium red to dull the green. Add size. Use a #4 brush and paint the trees, starting at the top of each and making deliberate alternating strokes coming down the trees. Don't smooth it out. This gives it texture.

This is what the side you are painting should look like.

Here is what the reverse should look like at this point.

Mix green for the grass, making it a little bit darker than the tree color using more Prussian blue and cadmium red. Also mix ¹/₄ inch of Shiva yellow with size. Using a ¹/₂-inch brush, paint the green as indicated. Then paint yellow on the rest of the grass with a #10 brush and blend the two together.

The reverse side looks like this.

For the sky, mix 1 inch of white with small amounts of Prussian blue and raw umber until it matches the blue in the picture; add size, mix well, and put in a cap. Then mix $1/2$ inch of white with a small amount of Indian yellow to match the picture; add size and put in a cap. Put a bit of white out on the palette. With a $1/2$-inch brush, paint blue at top of the glass down to the top of the taller house.

Now dip your finger in the white to make clouds (see page 37). The photo shows the reverse side.

With another $1/2$-inch brush, paint yellow in the area indicated. Then, while looking at the front of the glass, stroke across the back to blend blue and yellow.

Now finish the sky with blue, blending the yellow and blue. Let the glass dry for several days before framing.

Here is the finished piece from the front.

Doll with a Blue Dress

Here is another simple project that will give you practice with the basics—a primitive rag doll picture adapted from a contemporary theorem pattern. It will take you less than a week to complete and will brighten any little girl's bedroom or play area.

Allow the painting to dry for a full twenty-four hours after each day's work. Prepare a 7 x 9-inch piece of glass and set it up with the pattern (see pages 26–27).

Using a size 3/0 Rapidograph pen, draw all the lines in black except the hair. Be sure to hold the pen vertical at all times. The ink dries very quickly, but be careful not to smear it. A mistake can be removed easily with a damp paper towel.

When the ink lines are completed, mix ¼ inch of burnt sienna with size. Using a 10/0 liner brush, paint in the hair.

Mix a very small amount of white paint with size and put the small highlights in the eyes and nose. Remove the glass from the pattern.

Mix $\frac{1}{8}$ inch of lamp black with size and paint the bottom of the shoes and the shoe straps using a #2 brush. Rinse out the brush with mineral spirits so you can use it again.

Mix a small amount of Prussian blue, black, and white with size to match the color in the picture and use the 10/0 liner to paint the eyes and buttons. Clean the brush for reuse. Mix a very small amount of Shiva yellow medium with a tiny bit of burnt umber and size and paint the flower center and sock stripes. Rinse out the brush again. Mix a tiny amount of cadmium red pale with size and paint the nose and mouth with the 10/0 liner. Mix $\frac{1}{2}$ inch of white with size and use the #2 brush to paint the apron and ruffles at the neck, wrists, and pants bottoms.

Finally, mix a small amount of burnt umber for a glaze (see page 34). Using a #2 or #4 brush, paint behind the hair, shading off before the ends of the burnt sienna lines.

This is what the side you are painting on should look like at this point.

The reverse side, the front, should look like this.

Mix a small amount of burnt umber with a tiny bit of white with size; using a #2 brush, paint the shoe tops. Mix a small amount of Shiva yellow medium with a tiny bit of white and size and paint the socks with a #2 brush.

Your picture should now look like this.

Mix ¼ inch of white and a tiny bit of alizarin crimson with size to make flesh color to match the picture. Paint the face, neck, and hands. Then mix a small amount of medium green using Shiva yellow medium, Prussian blue, and cadmium red pale with size and paint the small leaf on the flower. Finally, for the flower, you will use two small amounts of paints, one white with size and one cadmium red pale with size. Using one #2 brush for red, paint the outside of one petal. Take another #2 brush for white and paint the inside of the petal with white. Holding the glass so you are looking at the front, carefully blend the white into the red with your white brush. Repeat on the other three petals, wiping out the white brush between petals. If you go outside the black lines, you can clean it with your touch-up brush and lighter fluid. Dip the touch-up brush in the lighter fluid, wipe it out on a paper towel and carefully clean off excess paint.

The next step is painting the dress. You will need two shades of blue. Mix ¹/₂ inch of white with tiny amounts of Prussian blue and raw umber. Add size. Match the color to the lighter shade of blue in the picture. Put half in a cap, and then add more Prussian blue and raw umber to match the darker color and put it in a cap.

Using a #4 brush, paint the darker color down both sides of one arm.

With another #4 brush, paint the lighter color down the middle.

Looking at the front of the glass, blend the light color into the darker color using long strokes. Use a very light touch on the brush.

Put the glass back down and repeat blending on the dress front, other arm, and skirt, finishing up with the ribbon and hair ties. You may want to use a smaller brush for these.

The side you're painting on should look like this.

Here is the reverse.

The last step on your glass is the background. Mix $1^1/_2$ inches of white with small amounts of Indian yellow and burnt umber with size, making the lighter top half of the glass. Cap $^2/_3$ of this mix, and then add more burnt umber to the remainder to match the bottom half of the glass.

Here is the finished piece from the front.

Paint the background color right over the doll using a $^1/_2$-inch brush for each color.

Let it dry several days before framing.

The Church with Weeping Trees

This church scene project will help you develop your skills in painted line work, stippling, shadowing, and other dimensional detailing. Review the Basic Skills section on making mountains, as you will be adding some here. The project will take you about a week to complete.

This project, like most others in the book, needs a full twenty-four hours to dry after each day's work.

Prepare an 8 x 10-inch piece of glass and set it up with the pattern (see pages 26–27).

Mix 1/2 inch of burnt umber with a tiny bit of black and add size (see page 41). Put it in a cap. Using the 10/0 brush, paint all line work.

With a 1/4-inch deerfoot stippler, stipple the umber in the trees and grass areas (see page 38). The stippler should be used with very little paint or it will make blobs.

Remove the glass from the pattern.

Mix burnt umber with size to make a glaze (see page 34). Use a #4 brush and apply glaze to the right side of the house, the front door, and the right side of the steeple.

Now start mixing the green for the grass and trees. Use 1 inch of Shiva yellow, add Prussian blue in small amounts until you get medium green, and then add a little cadmium red pale to match the picture. Add size and put ⅔ of the mix in a cap. Add more blue and red to the other ⅓ to match the darker green. Add a bit more size and put it in a cap. Now mix ¼ inch of Shiva yellow with size and put it in a cap. Put a small amount of burnt umber out on your palette.

Use the stippler to stipple the trees. Start in the middle with dark green, and then wipe out the brush. Move on further to the edges of the trees with the medium green, and wipe out the brush again. Then stipple the yellow along the edges of the trees.

Now start the grass. Using a ½-inch brush, paint the lighter green in the area indicated on the picture. Pick up a little burnt umber on the brush and pull it through the green along the top. Now paint the yellow with a #10 brush and stroke the green and yellow together to make a smooth blend.

Paint the bottom corner with the dark green and push a little up into the yellow under the umber stippling. Now go back and paint the hill with the dark green. Then take the yellow brush and pull it through the green to blend where you see it in the picture.

The side you are painting on should look like this.

Day 3

The red roofs are next. You will need two shades of red. Mix ¹/₄ inch of cadmium red and add a little white and size for the lighter shade. Take half of that mixture and add alizarin crimson to make the darker shade. Use a #4 brush and paint the entire steeple dark red.

Now paint the dark red on the roof where indicated on the picture. Use another #4 brush to paint the rest of the roof with the lighter color, just barely touching the dark red.

Mix ¹/₂ inch of white with size and put it in a cap. Mix ¹/₈ inch of Shiva yellow with a little white and size. With a #10 brush, paint the steeple house white, covering the umber glaze.

Use a #4 brush to pull yellow in where shown. Now paint the church with white from the umber side to where the yellow starts.

Paint the rest yellow. Use the white brush to blend the two colors together.

This is what the side you are painting on should look like.

Here is the reverse.

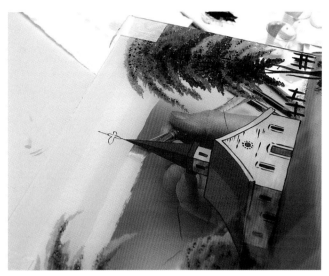

Repeat down the sky to where yellow should start.

We are now ready to paint the sky. To make the blue, mix 1 inch of white with small amounts of Prussian blue and raw umber to match the blue. Add size and put it in a cap. Mix 1 inch of white with a small amount of raw umber to match cloud streaks, add size, and put it in a cap. Now take ¹/₄ inch of white, add a tiny amount of Indian yellow and size, and put it in a cap. Finally, mix ¹/₈ inch of Prussian blue with ¹/₈ inch of raw umber (do not add size) and leave it on the palette.

Now paint the rest of the glass yellow with a ¹/₂-inch brush. Blend yellow and blue with your yellow brush.

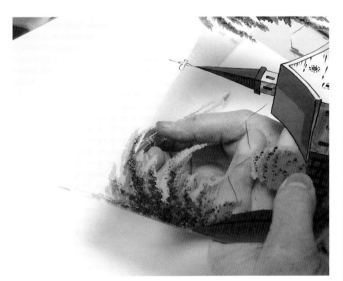

Using a ¹/₂-inch brush, paint the top blue. With a #10 brush, put on the next stroke with the off-white and blend, using long strokes.

Now you will paint the mountains. You will do the mountain on the red roof side of the church first. Then you will paint the one next to it. This will make one appear to be in front of the other. To do this, take the blue brush and pull the mountains through the yellow, making a deliberate sweep up and then down, looking at the front of the glass. Make as many strokes as needed to complete one mountain, and then go to the next (see page 37). Try not to restroke over these and each mountain will have its own character. Complete the mountain on the other side of the church.

Now take the stippling brush and dip it in the dark blue mixture on your palette, wipe most of it out, and then stipple the dark trees. Look at the front of the glass when you do this, so that you can tell what it looks like. Let the glass dry several days before framing.

Here is the side you are painting on.

Here is the finished piece from the front.

Three-Masted Schooner

Masted ships were a common theme in nineteenth-century art and design. This project will take about half a week and will give you practice with stroke work, blending, and making a sky-to-water horizon.

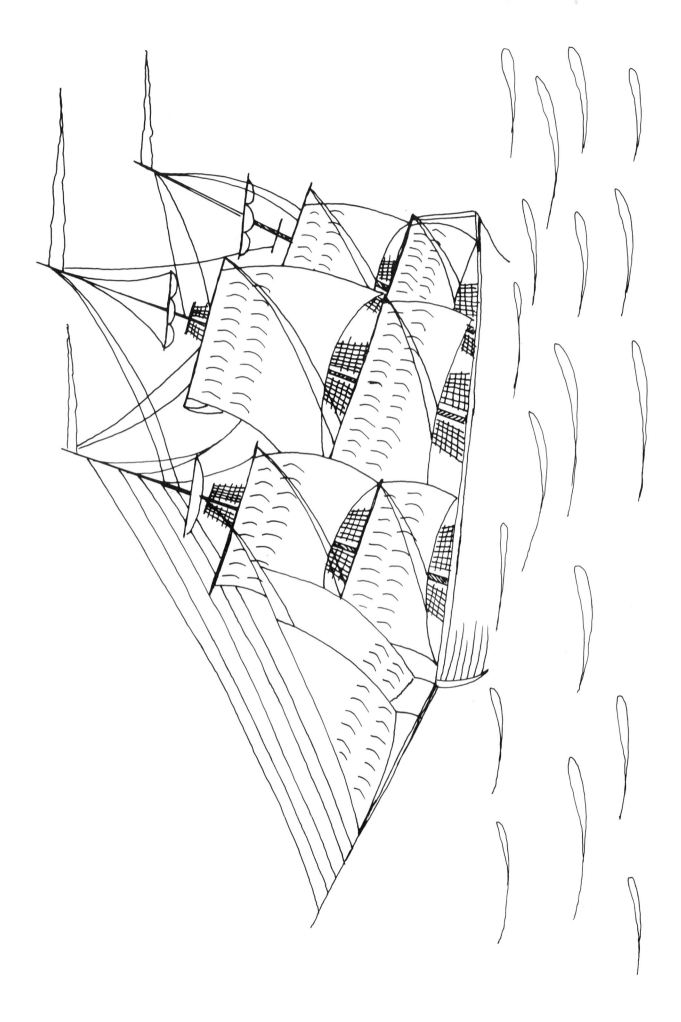

Allow the painting to dry for a full twenty-four hours after each day's work. Prepare an 8 x 10-inch piece of glass and set it up with the pattern (see pages 26–27).

Mix $1/4$ inch of burnt umber with a tiny bit of black, add size, and put the mixture in a cap. Paint all the line work with a 10/0 brush. Use a #2 brush to paint brown strokes at the bottom for the ocean waves. Then mix a tiny bit of cadmium red pale with size and paint the red flags. Now mix a tiny bit of Shiva yellow, Prussian blue, and cadmium red pale with size to make green for the flag on the right.

Mix a small amount of white with size and use a #2 brush to paint white strokes among the brown strokes in the water. Put a small amount of burnt sienna on the palette. Put size in a cap. Using a #10 brush, load with size, stroke one edge against the burnt sienna and blend through the brush to make a dark to light stroke. Make strokes across a sail, as shown in the picture. Repeat this for each sail, reloading the brush each time. Mix a tiny amount of burnt umber with size and paint the bottom of the boat. Then mix a tiny bit of cadmium red pale with size on the palette. Beside it, mix a tiny bit of Shiva yellow with size. With a 10/0 brush, paint red on the ship as shown. Then pull the yellow gently into the red.

Mix $\frac{1}{4}$ inch of white with size and use a #10 brush to paint all the sails and the boat over the glazes.

Here is what the front should look like at this point.

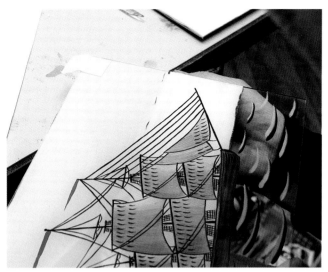

Mix ³/₄ inch of white with small amounts of Prussian blue and raw umber to match the top part of the sky; add size and put it in a cap. Mix ¹/₂ inch of white with a very small amount of Indian yellow to match the lower sky; add size and put it in a cap. Mix ¹/₄ inch of Prussian blue with an equal amount of raw umber; add size and put it in a cap. On the front of the glass, use a china marker to indicate where the horizon line will be. Using a ³/₄-inch brush, paint blue on the top one-third of the glass.

Use a ¹/₂-inch brush to paint yellow from the blue down to the horizon line. While looking at the front, reach carefully around the back and use the yellow brush to blend the blue and yellow, drawing the brush all the way across the glass.

You may need to hold the glass on the sides in the blue sky area while you work on the water. If you smudge the sky, go back and repaint it.

The side you are painting on will look like this. Let it dry for several days before framing it.

Use another ¹/₂-inch brush and paint the dark blue on the bottom of the glass. Now draw the dark blue water brush across the horizon line, just touching the yellow to create a soft horizon. Pick up a bit of raw umber on the water brush and pull in under the boat.

Here is the finished piece from the front.

Ocean Cottage in Gold

This picture of a cottage by the sea was adapted from an old design. The project will give you experience in using gold leaf on glass. You will be referring frequently to the gold leaf section in Basic Skills. You will also paint a sky with clouds. The project will take you less than a week to complete.

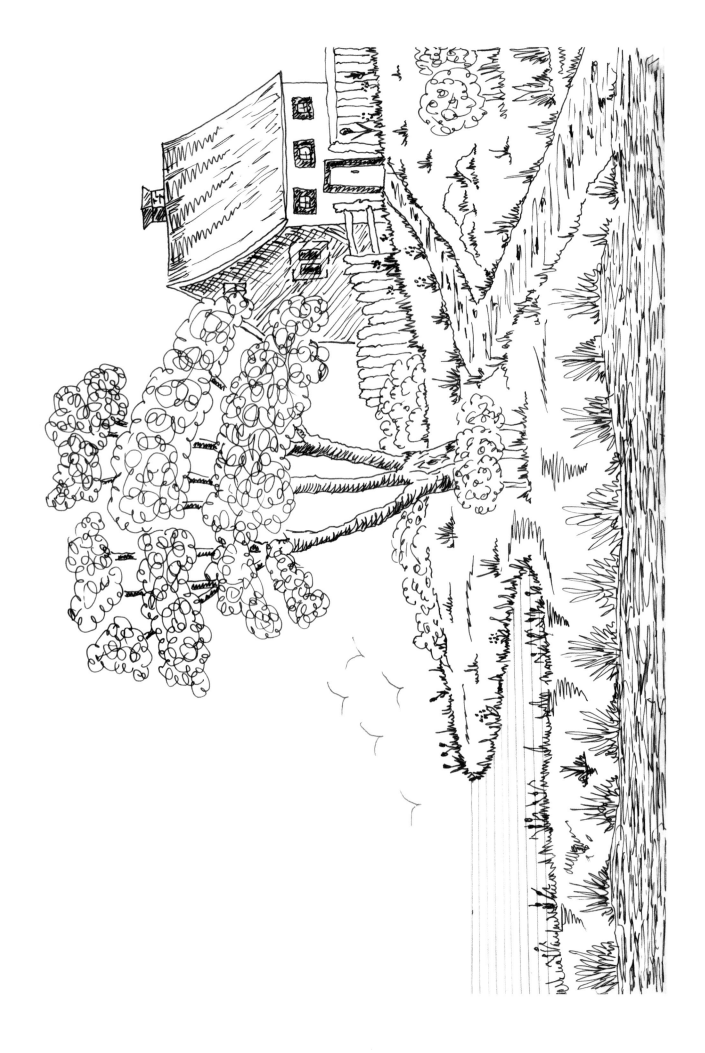

Prepare an 8 x10-inch piece of glass. You will need to trace the design on tracing paper. Photocopies don't work for gold leaf. Place the pattern on a piece of cardboard, so that you can see the design as you will when it is finished.

Follow the instructions for gold leafing in Basic Skills on page 40 to apply the first layer of gold leaf. Let it dry for a few hours. Then burnish the layer with a soft cotton pad. Apply the second layer of gold leaf and let it dry again (see page 43). Brush off excess gold, but do not burnish.

Lay the glass over the pattern, tab side up, and use a china marker to draw a line ¼ inch larger than the design. Draw an arrow pointing up to indicate the top.

Secure the pattern (now reversed) over gold leaf and place a piece of transfer paper in between. Trace the outlines onto the gold with a stylus.

Place the glass on a piece of black cardboard. Use a dulled #16 blade to etch the design. Do not etch the birds or water. Etch all the outlines first, then go back and begin shading. Don't shade any area too much, as you will have to shade the whole picture that way. You can always go back and shade more. You will be able to etch the gold for a week or two after applying it, but it is better to do it as soon as possible.

Put a small amount of Back Up Black in a cap. Use a #4 brush and cover all the gold leaf that will remain on the glass, going just over the etching lines at the edges. Change to a 10/0 brush to paint the birds and water lines, which are not etched. Let it dry for at least two hours. When the black is dry, wet a piece of cotton with ammonia and scrub off the excess gold. If the gold has been on the glass more than a few days, you may need to use a bit of whiting with the ammonia. Clean the glass with water and let dry.

The side you are working on should look like this. Let it dry for twenty-four hours.

Here is the reverse side.

Day 4

Mix $3/4$ inch of white with small amounts of Prussian blue and raw umber to match the blue sky color; add size, and put it in a cap. Mix $1/2$ inch of white with a small amount of Indian yellow, add size, and put it in a cap. Mix small amounts of Prussian blue and raw umber together, add size, and put it in a cap. Put a tiny bit of white on your palette.

Pick up a bit of white on your finger and push it through the blue to create clouds (refer to the technique in Basic Skills, page 37).

Using a $1/2$-inch brush, apply blue to the top half of the glass.

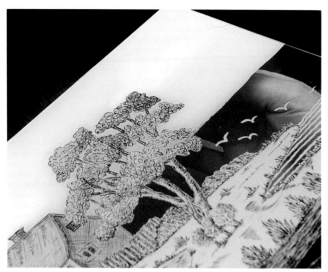

Now use another ¹/₂-inch brush and paint the yellow from the blue to the waterline. Watching the front of the glass, blend along the blue edge with the yellow brush.

Now use a #4 brush to paint the water with dark blue. Let the piece dry several days before framing it.

You can use your finger to blend this edge if you want it to look like clouds.

Merry Christmas

Here is an adaptation of a contemporary Christmas tinsel painting that uses a variety of mixed colors. The ornaments are all done with transparent colors so the foil sparkles through the glass. It includes a very simple, solid border. It will take you a week to paint the picture.

Allow the painting to dry for a full twenty-four hours after each day's work. Prepare an 8 x 10-inch piece of glass and set it up with the pattern.

Mix $^1/_4$ inch of lamp black with size and put it in a cap. Use a 10/0 brush and do all the line work (see page 30). Use the XCaliber striper to paint the oval stripe, gently twisting the striper as you go, so that the bristles will follow around the oval (see page 49).

Day 2

Mix a small amount of Indian yellow with size and paint the yellow bands on the ornaments.

Mix a tiny amount of alizarin crimson with size and paint the red bands and flower on the ornaments.

Mix ¹/₄ inch of Shiva yellow with small amounts of Prussian blue and cadmium red pale for the green leaves; add size and put it in a cap. Using a 10/0 brush, paint all the green leaves and pine needles. Using vermillion One Shot, paint the tiny berries with the end of a toothpick. Continue with the vermillion and a #10 brush to paint the entire area outside the black oval stripe. The painting should look like this when you finish for the day.

Day 3

Put ¹/₂ teaspoon of white One Shot in a cap and use a #10 brush to paint the background inside the oval. Use the 10/0 brush for the small spaces. You may paint over the green leaves and stems on the edges. Do not paint over the ornaments or the basket.

The side you are painting on should look like this.

Here's the reverse side.

Day 4

Mix a small amount of Prussian blue with a tiny amount of raw umber, add size, and paint the large blue ornament with a #2 brush. Then mix small amounts of alizarin crimson and Prussian blue for the purple ornaments, add size, and paint the ornaments. Now mix a tiny amount of Indian yellow with size and paint the two small yellow ornaments. Mix ¹⁄₄ teaspoon of rich-gold bronze powder with size and use a #10 brush to paint the basket. The painting should look like this.

Here's the reverse side.

Mix a small amount of alizarin crimson with size and paint the three red ornaments. Then mix tiny amounts of Prussian blue and raw umber with size and paint the two small blue ornaments. Mix a tiny amount of Indian yellow with size and paint the large yellow ornament. The painting should look like this.

Here's the reverse side.

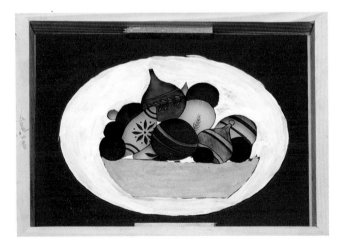

Mix small amounts of Indian yellow and Prussian blue for the green ornament, add size, and paint the ornament. Mix a tiny amount of white with enough size to make it transparent and paint the remaining two ornaments. White is an opaque color and needs more size in order to appear transparent. Let the painting dry several days before framing.

To create sparkle behind the transparent ornaments, crinkle aluminum foil and place it loosely in the frame behind the glass.

Fruit Basket

The fruit basket in this tinsel painting was adapted from a theorem painting, but the spirit is pure reverse glass, as you will be using transparent glazes and foil for special effects. It will take you a week to complete this project.

Allow the painting to dry for a full twenty-four hours after each day's work. Prepare an 8 x 10-inch piece of glass and set it up with the pattern.

Mix $1/4$ inch of burnt umber with a very small amount of lamp black, add size, and put it in a cap. Using the 10/0 brush, paint all the line work. The lines need to be fairly heavy for them to show through when the picture is finished.

Day 2

Mix 1 inch of white with enough Indian yellow to match the background color on the finished picture. Add size and put it in a cap. Using #4 and #10 brushes, paint the background. Use your 10/0 brush in small areas around the fruit. Mix $1/4$ inch of burnt umber with size and paint the table with a #10 brush.

Put a small amount of burnt umber on your palette and a bit of size in a cap. Now load a #10 brush with size. Touch one edge to the umber and dress the brush back and forth on the palette to get a dark to light graduated umber stroke (refer to side loading in Basic Skills, page 35). Now make a stroke down each section of the basket, creating the shadow. Check the design for placement. Redress for each stroke.

Mix a tiny amount of alizarin crimson with size. Use the 10/0 brush to make the dark red strokes on the flowers. Next, mix small amounts of alizarin crimson and Prussian blue together for the grapes, add size, and paint the grapes. Then mix a small amount of Indian yellow with alizarin crimson for the orange, add size, and paint the orange.

Mix $^1/_4$ inch of white with enough burnt umber for the basket, add size, and paint the basket using a #10 brush. Next mix $^1/_8$ inch of Prussian blue with a tiny amount of black, add size, and paint the blueberries with a #2 brush; these should be transparent so that the foil you add later for texture will show through. Now, mix $^1/_8$ inch of Indian yellow with size and put it in a cap. Use a 10/0 brush to paint the flower centers. Mix $^1/_8$ inch of alizarin crimson with size. Have two #4 brushes ready. Use one to paint Indian yellow in the center of the apple. Use the other to paint the outside edges of the apple with red. Then carefully blend the two colors together with the yellow brush (refer to Basic Skills, page 36). Repeat for the peach.

We will now paint the leaves, which are opaque. Mix $^1/_2$ inch of Shiva yellow with small amounts of Prussian blue and cadmium red pale to match the lighter shade on the leaves. Mix with size and put about $^1/_3$ of the mixture in a cap. Add more Prussian blue and red to match the darker color and put it in a cap. Use two #2 brushes and blend the larger leaves as shown, and then paint the smaller ones solid with the darker color.

Put a small amount of alizarin crimson on the palette and a small amount of size in a cap. Load a #4 brush with size and touch one edge in the alizarin. Dress the brush to get a dark to light gradual shading on it and paint the outside edges of the strawberries and flowers. Now mix small amounts of Indian yellow, Prussian blue, and alizarin crimson for the pears and add size. Mix a tiny amount of raw umber with the size. Using a #4 brush, paint umber in the neck area of one pear. With another #4 brush, paint the rest of the pear with green and blend with raw umber. Repeat this for the other pear.

Let the painting dry several days before framing it. Place a piece of crinkled aluminum foil loosely behind the glass in the frame. The finished piece should look like this.

Fruit Basket
with Red Drapes

In this project reproduced from an antique design, you will begin working on more complex border decorations. The picture will additionally give you experience in striping, blending, side-loading, and stippling. It takes about a week to complete.

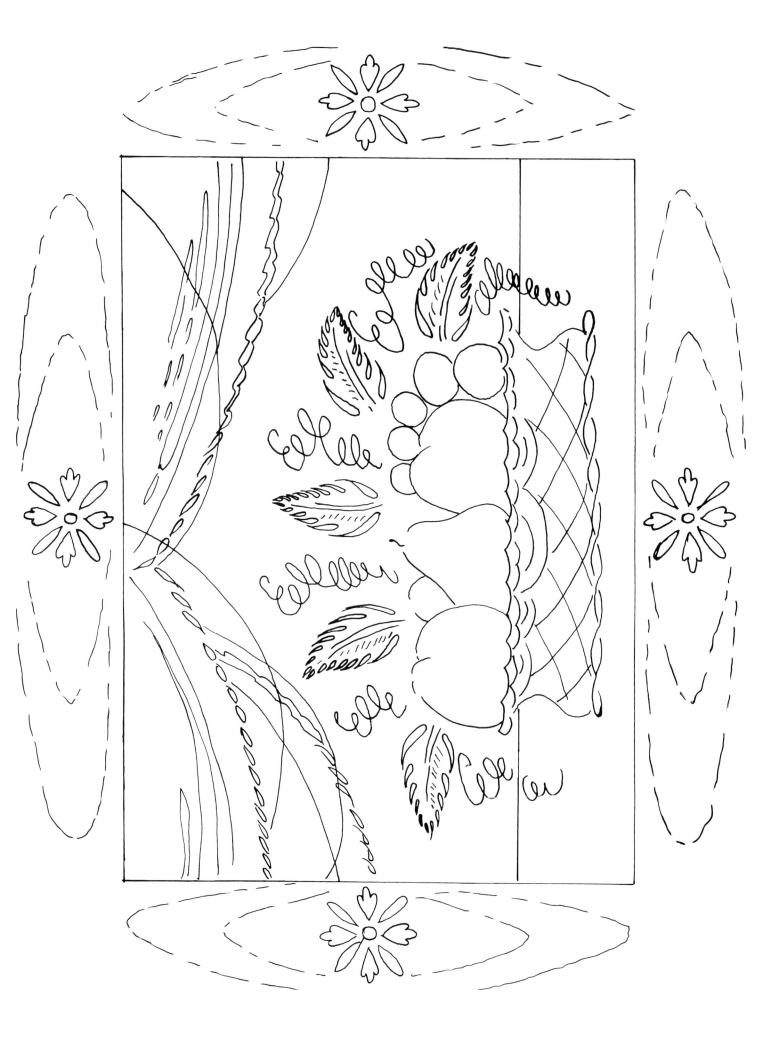

As with the previous projects, you should allow the painting to dry for twenty-four hours after each day's work. Prepare an 8 x 10-inch piece of glass and set it up with the pattern.

Mix $\frac{1}{2}$ inch of lamp black with size. Use your striper to paint the stripe on the glass (see page 48).

Day 2

Mix $\frac{1}{2}$ inch of lamp black with size and use your 10/0 brush to paint all the line work on the basket and the fruit. Mix $\frac{1}{4}$ inch of Shiva yellow with size and paint the yellow lines and strokes on the curtain, using the 10/0 brush.

The picture should now look like this.

Now take the palette knife and scoop a small amount of gold powder onto the palette and mix it with size. Paint the gold medallions on the border.

Mix ¼ inch of burnt umber with size and use a #4 brush to paint the lines of the curtains.

Now mix ¼ inch of Shiva yellow with small amounts of Prussian blue and cadmium red to make the green for the leaves. Add size and put it in a cap. Mix ¼ inch of Shiva yellow with size and put it in a cap. Using two #2 brushes, put the green on one leaf, and then add the yellow. Use the yellow brush to blend the two colors (see page 36).

Put a small amount of Prussian blue on your palette. Side load a #4 brush (see page 35), and paint the shadow on the grapes.

Clean up the edges of each leaf with a touch-up brush and lighter fluid. Repeat for all the leaves.

Now mix ¹/₄ inch of cadmium red with small amounts of Shiva yellow and burnt umber to make a burnt orange. Use the stippling brush and stipple the border where indicated. Use very little paint on the brush (see page 47).

Here's what the painting looks like at this point.

Here's the reverse.

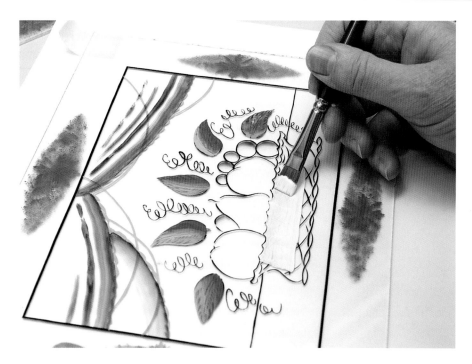

Mix $1/2$ inch of white with size and put it in a cap. Then mix $1/4$ inch of white with a small amount of lamp black for the edges of the basket. Add size and put it in a cap. Use a #10 brush to paint on the white. With a #2 brush, paint the gray on the sides and bottom. Blend the white and gray together using the white brush. Clean up with lighter fluid and the touch-up brush.

Mix $1/4$ inch of white with small amounts of Prussian blue and raw umber for the grapes. Add size and paint the grapes. Now mix $1/2$ inch of cadmium red with size and put it in a cap. Put a bit of burnt umber on the palette. Use a #10 brush and paint the bottom curtain red. Pick up a bit of umber on the brush and blend in along the bottom edge of the curtain. Repeat for the other curtains. Next, mix $1/4$ inch of Shiva yellow with a small amount of burnt umber for the second stipple color around the border. Add size and stipple the border as shown.

Mix $1/4$ inch of cadmium red with size and put it in a cap. Then mix $1/4$ inch of Shiva yellow with size and put it in a cap. Put a bit of burnt umber on your palette. Using a #4 brush, paint the red on the peach closest to the grapes. Tip the brush in umber and shade along the outer edge.

Now use another #4 brush and paint the rest of the fruit yellow. Blend the red with the yellow.

Clean up and then do the other two fruits the same way. Now mix 1 inch of white with a small amount of Indian yellow for the border and add size. Paint over the entire border using a $1/2$-inch brush. Here's the painting at this point.

The reverse side should look like this.

Mix ³/₄ inch of white with small amounts of Prussian blue and Shiva yellow for the top background and add size. Paint on the glass with a ¹/₂-inch brush, being careful not to paint over the three central pieces of fruit and the curtain. Now mix ¹/₂ inch of Shiva yellow with a small amount of white for the bottom background and add size. Mix ¹/₄ inch of lamp black with size. Paint the black shadow first with a #4 brush. Then paint the yellow with a #10 brush, being careful not to paint behind the basket. Blend the edges of the black and yellow just a little.

Let dry for several days before framing.

Here is the finished piece from the front.

Sailing Home

Now we move on to even more elaborate borders using stencils. This is a complex project that will take two weeks to complete. You will exercise just about every technique you've learned to this point, plus the dry-brush technique.

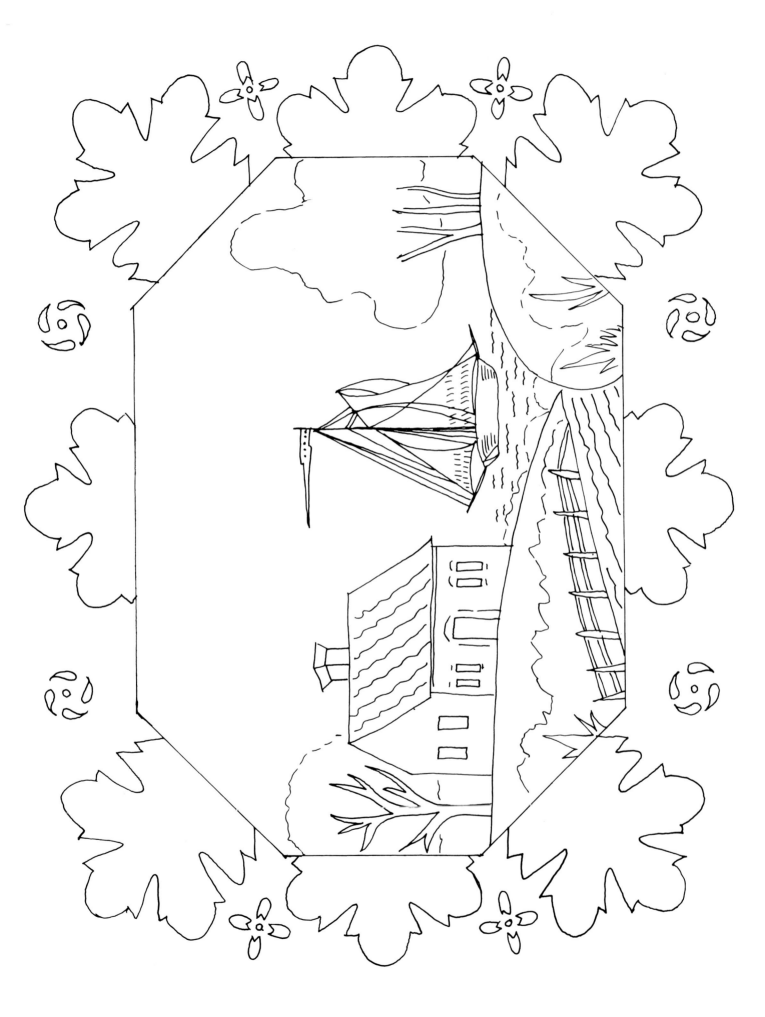

#1

Use this piece

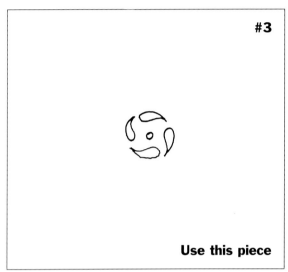

#3

Use this piece

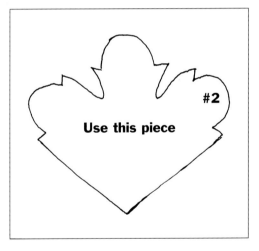

#2

Use this piece

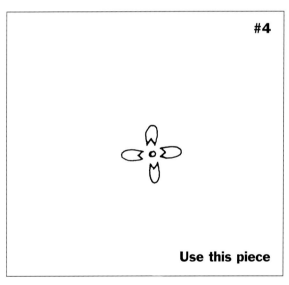

#4

Use this piece

Drying times will be longer after some of the steps in this project, so follow the instructions carefully. Trace the four stencils from the preceding page on Denril and cut them following the instructions on page 47. Prepare an 8 x 10-inch piece of glass and set it up with the pattern.

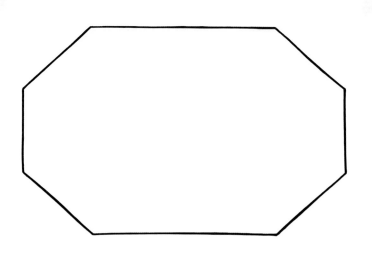

Paint the border stripe on the glass (see page 48). Let it dry for twenty-four hours.

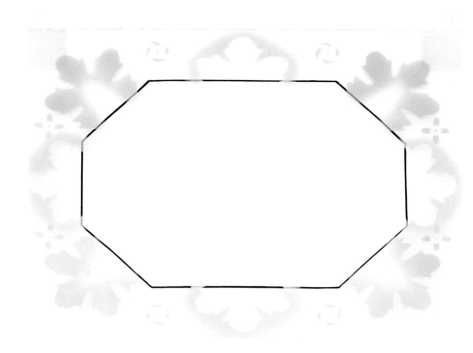

The next step is to stencil the border (see page 47). Use a tack cloth to remove any dust. Varnish the border, and then set it aside until the tack is ready, about two-and-a-half to three hours. The surface should be just dry enough so the Denril doesn't stick. Have the gold and silver powders ready. Start on the corners with the gold. Place the stencil matching the pattern under the glass and then slide a piece of black cardboard under the area to be stenciled. Polish brightly around the edges and shade off to the center. Repeat this on the other corners. Now do the small units in gold using the same procedure. The last four units are silver. Polish brightly all around the negative stencil; then shade off in a semicircle. Let it dry for forty-eight hours.

After the forty-eight hours have passed, clean the stenciled area with a soft rag and distilled water. Erase any bronze powders that have scattered away from the design with a soft pencil eraser. Dry carefully with a soft cloth. Let the glass sit for an hour or so to dry. Now varnish over the whole border. After forty-eight hours, varnish the border again. Let it dry for twenty-four hours.

Day 7

Now you're ready to start painting the picture. Mix $1/4$ inch of burnt umber with a tiny bit of black and size. Using the 10/0 liner, paint all the line work. Notice that the fence and grass in the stippled areas are not outlined. Let it dry for twenty-four hours.

Mix burnt umber with size and use the deerfoot stippler to stipple the trees and bushes on both sides.

Now dip the ⅛-inch angled shader in lighter fluid and wipe it on a paper towel.

Then pull the brush through the stippling, removing the paint to create the fence and grass clumps. Do umber stippling on the trees. Now remove the pattern from under the glass. Use a #2 brush to put umber glaze on the end of the house, the chimney, and the boat. To make the shading on the sails, side load your #4 brush with burnt umber and shade one side of each sail. Mix a tiny bit of white and size and put the dots in the flag using a toothpick.

Now put a small amount of fire red One Shot into a cap. Using a #4 brush, carefully fill in the area inside the silver stenciled border units.

Here's the reverse side.

Mix a teaspoon of medium green One Shot with a little chrome yellow One Shot and fire red One Shot and put it in a cap. Using the #2 brush, paint behind the entire gold corner units, being careful not to go past the edges. Let it dry for twenty-four hours. At this point, the picture should look like this.

Mix ¹/₄ inch of cadmium red pale with size and put it in a cap. Mix a smaller amount of white with size. Use a #4 brush for the red and paint the top part of the roof. Then use a #2 brush with white to paint the bottom half. Carefully blend the two colors together and then paint the red flag. Now mix a small amount of Shiva yellow with size and a small amount of burnt umber with size. Start at the bottom of the road with the burnt umber on a #2 brush and paint a stroke across the bottom. Next make a stroke of red above it and blend the two together. Repeat with yellow on a #4 brush, and then finish with white.

Clean up the edges of the road with a touch-up brush. Let it dry for twenty-four hours. The side you are painting on should look like this.

Mix ¹/₄ inch of white with size. Put small amounts of burnt umber and Shiva yellow on your palette. Use a #2 brush to paint the white on the sails, boat, house, and chimney. Touch the brush in the umber and stroke through the front of the house, watching from the front. Then do the same with the yellow. Take out a teaspoon of dark brown One Shot and paint the entire border. The picture should look like this.

Here's the reverse.

Start with ¹/₂ inch of Shiva yellow, mix in Prussian blue a little at a time to make medium green, and then add a little cadmium red to soften the green. Check the color to match the picture. Add size and put it in a cap. Mix ¹/₄ inch of Shiva yellow with size and put it in a cap. Use a #10 brush to apply green on one side of the grass. Using a #4 brush, apply yellow to the rest of the side and blend carefully. Repeat this sequence on the other grass area. Now paint the trees, green first and then blending yellow around the top edges.

Clean up and let it dry for twenty-four hours. Here's the side you're painting on.

Here's the reverse side.

The sky, mountains, and water are all done in one session. Start by mixing the blue. Use $3/4$ inch of white, and then add very small amounts of Prussian blue and raw umber until it matches the blue at the top of the sky Add size, and put it in a cap. Now use $1/2$ inch of white and add Indian yellow in small amounts until it matches the central part of the sky; add size, and put it in a cap. Using $1/4$ inch of white, add a tiny amount of alizarin crimson until it matches the bottom of the sky. Add size

and put it in a cap. Last, mix $1/4$ inch of white with black for the mountains, add size, and put it in a cap.

On the front of the glass, draw a line with a china marker at the horizon line, and indicate where the mountains will go. Return to the other side. Using your $1/2$-inch brushes, start at the top with blue and paint down as far as shown in the picture, then paint the yellow as indicated. Blend them together using long strokes to make a smooth blend. Now paint the pink down to the horizon line and blend the yellow and pink. Wipe out your blue brush and load it with gray. Looking at the front, pull the gray through the sky in an upward, then downward movement to form the mountain peak. Continue with smaller up and down strokes below the initial stroke to complete the mountain. Then complete the rest of the mountains the same way. Now take a paper towel and wipe off the paint below the horizon line. With the pink brush, paint the top part of the water. Pull it to just touch the bottom of the mountains to create the horizon line. Continue down the water, blending pink to yellow, then yellow to blue. Finally, get a little burnt umber on a #4 brush and gently pull in a shadow under the boat.

Here is the finished piece from the front. Let the painting dry for several days before framing it.

Gideon Resting

Here again you will be using stencils to create the fantastic border around this old design of man's best friend. And again, you will be using many of the more complex techniques you have learned so far. It will take you about a week and a half to finish it.

#1

Use this piece

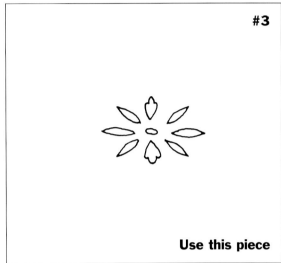

#3

Use this piece

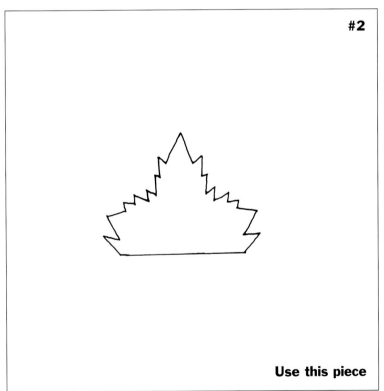

#2

Use this piece

#4

Use this piece

Drying times will be longer after some of the steps in this project, so follow the instructions carefully. Trace the four stencils from the preceding page on Denril and cut them following the technique in Basic Skills. You may also want to review the techniques for stenciling borders on page 47. Prepare an 8 x 10-inch piece of glass and set up the pattern. Mix ¼ inch of lamp black with size and stripe the glass with the XCaliber striper. Clean up the corners with lighter fluid and the ⅛-inch angled shader. Let it dry for twenty-four hours.

Day 2

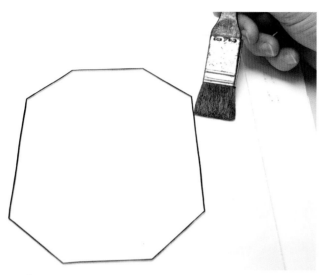

Mix ⅛ inch of burnt umber with a tiny bit of lamp black, add size, and put it in a cap. Use a 10/0 brush and paint all the line work. Use a 1-inch sponge brush to varnish the border of the glass, going halfway over the stripe. Let the varnish dry for a few hours, until the Denril doesn't stick.

Slide black cardboard under the glass. Using richgold powder and a finger pad, stencil the corner. Repeat this process for the other three corners. Next, use the richgold to place and stencil the eight small flowers.

Place the corner stencil down where indicated on the pattern.

Now finish the last four leaves with silver powder. Always have black cardboard under the glass when stenciling. Let it dry for twenty-four hours.

At this stage, the side you are work-ing on should look like this.

Day 3

Mix $^{1}/_{4}$ inch of burnt umber with size and put it in a cap. Take a #4 brush and dip it in the paint, and then brush most of the paint out on the palette. Now paint the dog's fur in short strokes. Leave areas open on the dog for white markings, such as on the head and mane in this de-sign. Paint the bottom of the stool. Mix a tiny bit of white and alizarin crimson with size and paint the tongue. Mix a tiny bit of lamp black with size and paint the eyes. Let it dry for twenty-four hours.

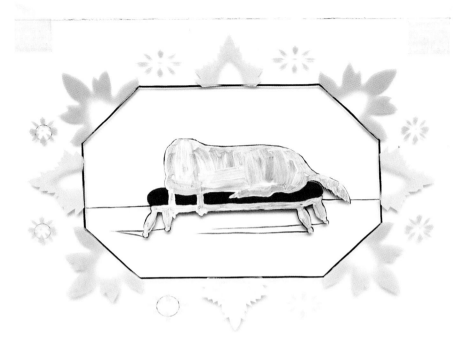

Mix a small amount of white and size. Paint behind the dog and the bottom of the stool. Mix $1/8$ inch of cadmium red pale with a tiny bit of burnt umber, add size, and paint the cushion. Using a cotton knit rag dampened with distilled water, clean only the stenciled border. When finished, wipe it dry. Wait one hour; then varnish the border over the stencils. Let it dry for forty-eight hours.

Day 6

Varnish the border a second time and let it dry for twenty-four hours.

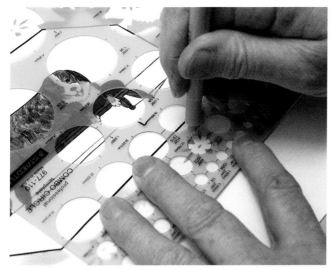

Turn the glass to the front and use a circle template and a pointed Sharpie to make circles on each of the eight small flowers.

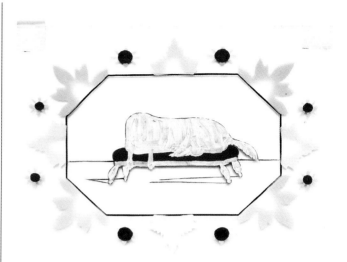

Here's the painting so far.

Using fire red One Shot, paint the circles on the varnished side of the glass. Let it dry for twenty-four hours.

Here's the reverse side.

Paint behind the entire border with dark brown One Shot. Let it dry for twenty-four hours.

Day 9

Mix ¹/₂ inch of white with small amounts of Prussian blue and raw umber for the blue background. Add size and put it in a cap. Mix ¹/₄ inch of white with a small amount of Indian yellow for the lower part of the background, add size, and put it in a cap. Using a ¹/₂-inch brush, paint the blue background just below the line where the wall meets the floor in the picture. Use another ¹/₂-inch brush and pull a bit of yellow through the blue just above the dog on the left and blend. Paint the rest of the background with the yellow and blend it along the edge with the blue.

Here is the finished piece from the front. Let it dry for several days before framing.

Flower Gathering

We go from animal to human figures in this project. Here you will learn to mix paint for flesh tones and blushing, perfect your blending skills to create a colorful dreamland sky, and hone your stenciling and stippling techniques to make a detailed floral border. It will take you a week and a half to complete the work.

#1

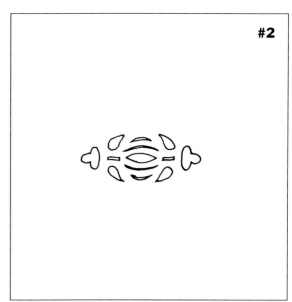

#2

Day 1

After each day's work, allow the painting to dry for twenty-four hours. Trace the two stencils above on Denril and cut them following the technique in Basic Skills. You may also want to review the techniques for stenciling borders on page 47. Prepare an 8 x 10-inch piece of glass and set up with the pattern.

Mix ¹/₄ inch of burnt umber with size and use the XCaliber striper to stripe the glass.

As you approach the corner, twist the brush slightly in your fingers so that the bristles go more easily around the curve.

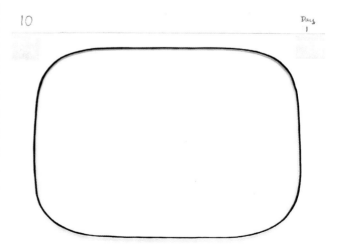

Once you are around the curve, reload the brush to straighten the bristles and continue.

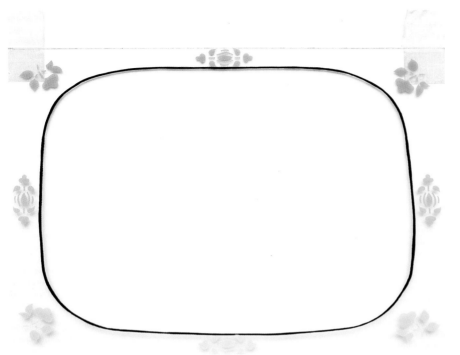

Use a 3/4-inch brush and varnish the border, going halfway over the stripe. When the varnish is almost dry, put the corner stencil in place, slide black cardboard underneath the glass, and stencil the design with richgold bronze powder. Repeat the process for the other corners; using the other stencil, apply the gold to the center units.

Day 3

Mix 1/2 inch of burnt umber with a tiny amount of lamp black, add size, and put it in a cap. Use a 10/0 brush and do all the line work.

Mix a tiny amount of burnt umber with size and paint the glaze on the hair and eyelids. Next mix tiny amounts of cadmium red pale with alizarin crimson; add size and paint the red details on the three flowers and the butterfly. Mix tiny amounts of white, Prussian blue, and raw umber for the shoes; add size, and then paint the shoes. Then pull a bit of white without size through the area indicated with a #2 brush. Clean the stenciled border with distilled water and dry. Use a #10 brush and paint varnish over the stencil designs only, not the entire border.

Now mix Prussian blue and raw umber for the blue glaze and add size. Use a #10 brush to apply the glazes to the grass, trees, basket leaves, hat ribbon, dress ribbon, and small leaves on the hat and flowers. Use a fairly dry brush to paint the glaze so it isn't solid.

Mix tiny amounts of Shiva yellow and burnt umber with size and paint over the hair and the centers in the three flowers. The side you are painting on should look like this.

blend. Mix $1/2$ inch of Shiva yellow with small amounts of Prussian blue and cadmium red pale for the grass and trees, add size, and put it in a cap. Paint the grass and trees using a #10 brush. Use a smaller brush to paint the belt, bow, and flower leaves. Then use a #10 brush to put a second coat of varnish over the stencils on the border. When you finish for the day, the side you are working on should look like the picture at left.

Next, mix a tiny bit of white with size. Put a tiny bit of Shiva yellow and black on the palette. Paint the white on the three flowers and the butterfly with a #2 brush. Pull a little black through the butterfly's wings, and then do the same with a little yellow, watching on the front of the glass. Mix a small amount of Shiva yellow with a tiny bit of raw umber for the hat and add size. Divide in two parts and add more raw umber to one part. Paint the front half of the hat with the lighter yellow, and then paint the rest with the darker color and

Here's the reverse side.

Mix a small amount of white with a tiny amount of burnt sienna for the flesh color, add size, and put it in a cap. Paint the face and neck. Put a bit of alizarin crimson on your brush and push in color for the lips and blend in the cheek. Paint each hand and blend a bit of alizarin crimson along the bottom edge. Mix a tiny bit of white and size on your palette. Paint the basket and blend in the yellow and red where shown. Now mix $1/4$ inch of Shiva yellow with cadmium red pale and burnt umber for stippling and add size. Use the $1/4$-inch stippling brush and stipple (see page 32) as shown behind the stencil units.

Mix ¹/₄ inch of white with size and put half in a cap. Mix a small amount of lamp black in the other half for the dress and put it in a cap. Use two #4 brushes and start with the sleeve above the basket. Paint white and gray and then blend. Now in the following order paint the bodice, the other sleeve, the dress, and the socks. Mix ¹/₄ inch of Shiva yellow with Prussian blue and cadmium red pale for the green stippling, add size, and stipple the border where shown. The painting should look like this at the end of the day.

Here's what the reverse looks like.

Mix ¹/₄ inch of white with Prussian blue and raw umber for the blue in the sky; it should be very dark. Add size and put it in a cap.

Mix ¹/₂ inch of white with alizarin crimson for the pink in the sky; add size, and put it in a cap. Mix ¹/₄ inch of white and Indian yellow for the yellow in the sky, add size, and put it in a cap. Put a small amount of lamp black on the palette. Use a #10 brush and paint the blue. Use a ¹/₂-inch brush and paint the pink. Avoid painting over the lady. Use the pink brush to blend the blue and pink. Use a ¹/₂-inch brush to paint the yellow. Use the yellow brush to blend the pink and yellow. Pick up a bit of black on the yellow brush and pull the dark trees into the yellow sky. Be sure to check on the front to ensure your trees are pleasing to the eye. Clean up any intrusions on the border with lighter fluid and the ¹/₈-inch shader. Mix 1 teaspoon of white One Shot with a small amount of chrome yellow One Shot for the border color. Paint the border with a #10 brush.

Here is the finished piece from the front. Let it dry for several days before framing it.

The Dance

Now we add gold leafing to the border as you continue to use all the skills you've learned for this old reproduction of a woman stepping merrily. It will take a week to complete the project. Allow the painting to dry for twenty-four hours after each day's work.

Prepare an 8 x 10-inch piece of glass with tabs on it. Lay the glass with the tab side up on the pattern, which at this point is not reversed, and draw a circle ¹/₄ inch outside the area with a china marker where the gold leaf border designs will go. Follow the directions on page 41 for making size and laying the gold leaf. Stand the glass on the holder with the marked side away from you.

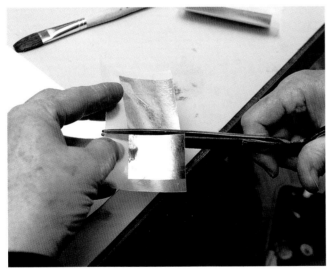

Cut your mounted sheet of gold leaf in quarters. Remember to rub the scissors with rouge paper. Apply two layers of gold in the four areas you have marked. When the second coat is dry, polish lightly with cotton, then take your tracing—now reversed—and lay it over the glass and fasten it with tape. Slide a piece of the black graphite paper under the tracing. Using a stylus, trace the circles. Make sure the graphite paper is on the side so that it leaves a tracing on your gold leaf. If you have a circle template, use it to make the circles. Now remove the tracing and graphite paper. Slide a piece of black cardboard under the glass and use the circle

template and stylus to etch the circles. Then use the craft knife with a dull #16 blade to etch the shadows. When you have finished etching, take a #2 brush and a small amount of Back Up Black to cover the etched part of your gold leaf, going just over the outside lines. Put white cardboard under the glass or hold it up to the light to make sure you cover all the etching lines. Let it dry for an hour. Using a piece of cotton and ammonia, carefully remove all the excess gold.

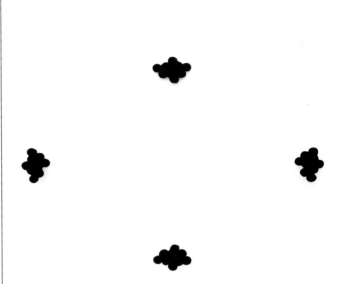

The black covers the parts you want to keep.

The front should look like this.

Now mount the pattern. Mix $\frac{1}{4}$ inch of lamp black with size and fully load the striping brush. Paint the border stripes.

Mix lamp black with size and use the 10/0 brush to paint in the lines for the girl. Then mix $\frac{1}{4}$ inch of burnt umber with size and paint the lines for the curtains. Using the stippling brush, stipple the umber around the gold leaf on the border. Make sure to use very little paint on your stippling brush. Remove the glass from the pattern.

Mix ¼ inch of Shiva yellow with size and use a #4 brush to paint the yellow on the curtains. Use the 10/0 brush to paint yellow on the sash, the wreath, and the hair. Mix ¼ inch cadmium red pale with size and use the 10/0 brush to paint the wreath and lips. Now add some alizarin crimson to the red paint to make a darker red and use a #4 brush to paint the dress. Put yellow in the areas indicated and blend it lightly. Now use your stippling brush and stipple the darker red on the border as shown.

Day 5

Mix ½ inch of cadmium red with size and put it in a cap. Mix ¼ inch of white with size and put it in a cap. Put a small amount of the burnt umber on your palette. With the #10 brush, paint the area of the top curtain with red.

Use a #4 brush with burnt umber on it and draw it through along the edge to make a shadow.

Using a #4 brush, add the white and then blend the white and red.

With the umber brush, make a few streaks through each curtain. Now paint the rest of the curtains the same way.

Next mix $1/4$ inch of white with a small amount of burnt sienna and size to make flesh. Paint one arm with the #2 brush, then pick up a tiny bit of burnt sienna on your brush and blend in the shadows. Always check blending on the front, as it does look different. Do the other arm the same way and then paint the face. Pick up a tiny bit of alizarin crimson on your brush and blush her cheeks. Now mix $1/4$ inch white with size and have a bit of lamp black on your palette. Use a #4 brush and paint the apron, then get a tiny bit of black on the brush and blend in to create shadows. Paint the socks the same way. Mix $1/4$ inch of Shiva yellow with small amounts of Prussian blue and cadmium red to make a dark green; add size, and put it in a cap. Use your 10/0 brush to paint the green on the wreath. Then use the stippling brush to stipple the green on the border.

Here's the front of the glass at this point.

Mix $1/4$ inch of white with tiny amounts of Prussian blue and raw umber to make the color for the blouse; add size. Paint the blouse with a #2 brush, then get a tiny bit of white on the brush and shade the sleeves and the front of the blouse. Add more blue to the mixture to paint the shoes. Put out 1 inch of white and add a small amount of Indian yellow and size and put it in a cap. Use a $1/2$-inch brush and paint the entire border.

The front looks like this.

Mix ½ inch of white with enough Shiva yellow and a little burnt umber for the top background color. Add size and put it in a cap. Mix ¼ inch of white with small amounts of Prussian blue and Shiva yellow for the bottom background color. Add size and put it in a cap. Use the ½-inch brushes to apply the two colors. Blend softly.

Here is the finished piece from the front. Let it dry several days before framing.

The Old Mill

This scene, taken from an antique design, uses most of the essential skills for
the craft of reverse glass painting. The project takes a week to complete.
Allow the painting to dry for twenty-four hours after each day's work.

Prepare an 8 x 10-inch piece of glass with tabs on it. Lay the glass with the tab side up on the pattern. Use a china marker to draw lines on both sides of the border, adding an extra $1/4$ inch. Refer to page 40 for instructions on laying gold leaf.

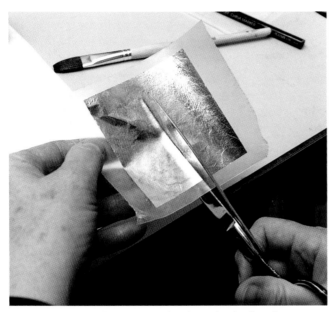

Cut the mounted pieces in thirds to fit the border area.

Apply the size and lay the gold across the top, down each side, and across the bottom.

Do the second coat, including etching, backing, and washing off the excess gold leaf. The glass will look like this at the end of the work session.

Set up the glass with the pattern on cardboard. Mix $1/4$ inch of lamp black with size and use your XCaliber striper to stripe the glass along the inner edge of the gold leaf border. Using your 10/0 brush, paint the black shadows in the outside edges of the gold leaf border, as shown in red on the pattern. Mix $1/2$ inch of burnt umber with a tiny amount of lamp black, add size, and put it in a cap. Using your 10/0 brush, paint all the line work. Use a bridge so you don't get your hand in the black paint.

Here's the front at this point.

Mix ½ inch of burnt umber with size and put it in a cap. Using a #2 or #4 brush, paint the umber washes on the houses, the mill wheel, trees, fences, and the man. Mix a small amount of Shiva yellow with size and use a stippler to stipple yellow on the leaf piles and bushes. Mix a tiny amount of Prussian blue and raw umber with size and paint the windows. Mix ¼ inch of cadmium red pale with ⅛ of alizarin crimson, add size, and paint every other space in the gold leaf border. Mix ¼ inch of Shiva yellow with small amounts of Prussian blue and cadmium red for the green in the border. Add size, and paint the remaining spaces on the border

Here's what the front looks like at the end of the session.

Mix a tiny bit of lamp black with size, a bit thinner than usual, and paint a transparent glaze on the rocks and arch. Mix a tiny amount of cadmium red and burnt umber with size and paint the center of the mill wheel. Mix $1/2$ inch of Shiva yellow with small amounts of Prussian blue and cadmium red for the lighter tree color. Add size and put half of the light green in a cap. Add more blue and red to the rest to match the darker trees and put it in a cap. Using #4 brushes, paint light trees first, and then paint the remaining trees, executing the darker parts first and then the lighter colors where indicated. Also paint the shutters on the large house. Mix a tiny amount of Prussian blue and raw umber with size and paint a transparent glaze on the front of the large house.

Here's the front.

Mix ¼ inch of white with size and paint the houses, fence, tree trunk, rocks, mill wheel, and man. Mix a bit of the white with a tiny amount of Prussian blue and black to make the lighter blue of the creek. Add a bit more size. Take half of this mixture and add more black to match the bottom part of the creek. Using #4 brushes, start at the top of the creek with white, and then add lighter blue and blend. Add darker blue at the bottom and blend into the lighter blue. Blending should work up and down the creek to create movement.

Mix a tiny amount of lamp black and size. Use a stippler to stipple the black trees. Mix ¼ inch of white with a small amount of raw umber for the outer border. Add size and paint the outer border.

Here's the front of the picture.

Mix ¹/₄ inch of Shiva yellow with small amounts of Prussian blue and cadmium red for the grass; add size, and put it in a cap. Mix a small amount of Shiva yellow with size and put it in a cap. Using a ¹/₂-inch brush, paint the grass, then pick up a bit of the yellow and pull it through the green where indicated. Look at the front of the glass to make sure it looks the way you want it to. Mix ¹/₂ inch of white with small amounts of Prussian blue and raw umber for the sky, add size, and put it in a cap. Now mix ¹/₄ inch of white with a tiny amount of Indian yellow for the yellow in the sky, add size, and put it in a cap. Put a tiny bit of alizarin crimson on your palette. Using ¹/₂-inch brushes, paint the blue and yellow and blend them together. Pick up a bit of alizarin crimson on the yellow brush and pull it through the very bottom of the sky.

Here is the finished piece from the front. Let dry several days before framing.

American Eagle in Gold

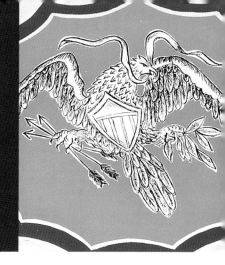

To finish, here's a spectacular project for those who have mastered etching skills. This classic Americana symbol will take you about a week to complete.

Prepare an 8 x 10-inch piece of glass with tabs. You must trace the design on tracing paper; photocopies don't work for gold leafing. Place the pattern on a piece of cardboard, so that you see the design as it will look when finished.

Lay the glass over the pattern, tab side up. With a china marker, draw a line $1/4$ inch larger than the design. Mark an arrow pointing up on the inside. Now follow the instructions from Basic Skills section (page 40) for laying gold leaf; then let it dry for a few hours. Burnish the gold leaf with a soft cotton pad. Apply the second layer of gold leaf. Let it dry again. Brush off the excess gold; do not burnish.

Secure the reversed pattern over the gold leaf and place a piece of transfer paper in between.

Trace the design onto the gold with a stylus and then remove the pattern and transfer the paper.

Place the glass on a piece of black cardboard.

Use a dulled #16 blade to etch the design. Do not etch the outside roping or the oval stripes around the eagle. Etch all the outlines first, then go back and begin shading. Don't shade any area too much at first; you can always go back and shade more. This may take more than one day's work.

Put a small amount of Back Up Black in a cap. Use a 10/0 brush to cover the design just over the etching lines. Paint stripes around the eagle and the roping around the edge. This will also take several hours to complete; it doesn't need to be done all at once.

When the black is dry, wet a piece of cotton with ammonia and scrub off the excess gold. If the gold has been on the glass more than a few days, you may need to use a bit of whiting with the ammonia.

Mix $1/4$ inch of Shiva yellow with small amounts of Prussian blue and lamp black for the color between the stripes surrounding the eagle. Add size and paint between the stripes with a 10/0 brush.

Mix $1/4$ inch of white with small amounts of Prussian blue and lamp black for the area behind eagle; add size and paint the area. Mix 1 inch of white with a small amount of Indian yellow for the outer background, add size, and paint the remainder of the glass using a $1/2$-inch brush.

Here is the finished piece from the front. Let dry several days before framing.

SUPPLIES AND RESOURCES

The Art Store
Commercial Art Supply
935 Erie Boulevard East
Syracuse, NY 13210
1-800-669-2787
www.commercialartsupply.com
Paints

Art Supply Warehouse
6104 Maddry Oaks Ct.
Raleigh, NC 27616
1-800-995-6778
www.aswexpress.com
Paints

Dick Blick Art Materials
P.O. Box 1267
Galesburg, IL 61402
1-800-828-4548
www.dickblick.com
Paints

Eastwood Company
263 Shoemaker Road
Pottstown, PA 19464
1-800-345-1178
www.eastwoodco.com
One Shot paints, Mack Xcalliber 0000
striper brush (catalog #37184)

Hofcraft
P.O. Box 72
Grand Haven, MI 49417
1-800-828-0359
www.hofcraft.com
Paints, brushes

Michael's
www.michaels.com
Cutter Bee retractable knife

New York Central Art Supply
62 Third Street
New York, NY 10003
1-800-950-6111
www.nycentralart.com
Gold leaf supplies

Pearl Fine Art Supplies
1033 East Oakland Park Blvd.
Fort Lauderdale, FL 33334
1-800-451-7327
www.pearlpaint.com
Denril, bronze lining powders

Scharff Brushes
P.O. Box 746
165 Commerce Drive
Fayetteville, GA 30214
1-888-724-2733
www.artbrush.com
Brushes

BIBLIOGRAPHY

Miniature reverse glass, measuring 2 x 3 inches and done on very thin glass and framed with copper foil. This piece can be used as an ornament, magnet, or a pin.

Bailey, Chris H. *Two Hundred Years of American Clocks and Watches*. Englewood Cliffs, NJ: Prentice-Hall, 1975.

Binnington, Frances. "Reverse Painting and Gilding Behind Glass." *The Decorator* 48, no. 2 (Spring 1994): 6.

Diston, William H., and Robert Bishop. *The American Clock: A Comprehensive Pictorial Survey, 1723–1900.* New York: E. P. Dutton, 1976.

Dworetsky, Lester, and Robert Dickstein. *Horology Americana*. Roslyn Heights, NY: Horology Americana, 1972.

Emery, Margaret J. *Techniques in Reverse Glass Painting.* Pittsfield, MA: Quality Printing, 1991.

Foley, Paul J. "Boston State House on Glass." *The Decorator* 58, no. 2 (Fall 2004): 4.

———. "Naval Battle Scenes from the War of 1812 on American Clocks." *The Decorator* 59, no. 1 (Spring 2005): 12.

———. *Willard's Patent Time Pieces: A History of the Weight-Driven Banjo Clock, 1800-1900.* Norwell, MA: Roxbury Village Publishing, 2002.

Hutchings, Dorothy. "Reverse Glass Paintings for Clocks and Mirrors." *The Decorator* 17, no. 2 (Spring 1963): 7.

Murray, Maria. "The Reverse Painted Glass 'Paris Plate' of the Corning Museum of Glass." *The Decorator* 19, no. 2 (Spring 1965): 8.

Pomeroy, Ingerid. "The $5.00 Bonanza." *The Decorator* 41, no. 2 (Spring 1987): 18.

Robinson, Roger W., and Herschel B. Burt. *The Willard House and Clock Museum and the Willard Family Clockmakers*. Columbia, PA: NAWCC, 1996.

Ryser, Frieder, *Reverse Painting on Glass: The Ryser Collection*. Edited and translated by Rudy Eswarin. Corning, NY: Corning Museum of Glass, 1992.

———. "Techniques of Reverse Painting on Glass: An Historical Overview." *The Decorator* 48, no. 2 (Spring 1994): 6.

Servino, Lucinda Burleigh. "William Bennet Fenn's Clock Glasses." *The Decorator* 38, no. 2 (Spring 1984): 4.

Smith, Esther. "Looking Glasses." *The Decorator* 25, no. 1 (Fall 1970): 13.

Weller, Gartley G. "Lemuel Curtis and Joseph Nye Dunning, American Clockmakers." *The Decorator* 28, no. 2 (Spring 1974): 4.